Test Your
Professional English

Medical

Alison Pohl
Series Editor: Nick Brieger

ALFONSO P. ONG

PENGUIN ENGLISH

Pearson Education Limited
Edinburgh Gate
Harlow
Essex CM20 2JE, England
and Associated Companies throughout the world.

ISBN 978-0-582-45147-6

First published 2002

Ninth impression 2011

Text copyright © Alison Pohl 2002

Designed by typeset by Pantek Arts Ltd, Maidstone, Kent
Test Your format devised by Peter Watcyn-Jones
Illustrations by Roger Fereday, Gillian Martin and Mark Watkinson
Printed in China
SWTC/09

Acknowledgements
I am truly grateful to Roland Koerner, MD, MRCPath for many things in life, but as far as this book is concerned I would like to express my grateful thanks for his valuable time and expertise without which this book would not have been possible. I would also like to express my grateful thanks to my old friend Jane Patterson, RN, RM for invaluable assistance and guidance with some of the material. To Nick Brieger, our faithful series editor, and Helen Parker and the team at Penguin Longman I would also like to say a heartfelt thank you.

Published by Pearson Education Limited in association with Penguin Books Ltd, both companies being subsidiaries of Pearson plc.

For a complete list of the titles available from Penguin English please visit our website at www.penguinenglish.com, or write to your local Pearson Education office or to: Penguin English Marketing Department, Pearson Education, Edinburgh Gate, Harlow, Essex CM20 2JE.

Contents

To the student

Perhaps you are studying medicine or training to work as a specialist in a medical field. Perhaps you are working in a hospital or medical centre in an English speaking country or perhaps you need English to communicate with patients and colleagues from other countries. Whatever your background, the tests in this book will help you improve your English. You can check your knowledge of key vocabulary and essential expressions and see how these terms are used. This will help you to communicate more effectively and confidently in your work or in your studies.

The book has been divided into eight sections. The first two sections provide an introduction to general medical terms and concepts. The other six sections cover different medical areas from patient history and hospitals to medical conditions. You may choose to work through the book from beginning to end or may find it more useful to select chapters according to your interests and needs.

Many tests also have tips (advice) on language, language learning and professional information. Do read these explanations and tips: they are there to help you.

To make the book more challenging and more fun, many different kinds of tests are used, including sentence transformation, gap-filling, word families, multiple choice and crosswords. There is a key at the back of the book so that you can check your answers; and a word list to help you revise key vocabulary.

Vocabulary is an important part of language learning and this book will help you to develop your specialist vocabulary. When you are learning vocabulary, notice how words are used (grammar) and when they are used (context). Perhaps you only need to recognise certain items of vocabulary when you read or hear them but if you need to be able to use them yourself at a later date, practise making sentences of your own. The tests in this book will help you check what you know and increase your knowledge of new concepts and terms in a structured and systematic way.

Alison Pohl

The full series consists of:

Test Your Professional English: Accounting	Alison Pohl
Test Your Professional English: Business General	Steve Flinders
Test Your Professional English: Business Intermediate	Steve Flinders
Test Your Professional English: Finance	Simon Sweeney
Test Your Professional English: Hotel and Catering	Alison Pohl
Test Your Professional English: Law	Nick Brieger
Test Your Professional English: Management	Simon Sweeney
Test Your Professional English: Marketing	Simon Sweeney
Test Your Professional English: Medical	Alison Pohl
Test Your Professional English: Secretarial	Alison Pohl

1 Parts of the body

Label the parts of the body. Choose from the following. Some have been done
for you.

forehead	2
chest	12
big toe	28
knee	26
cheek	7
palm	21
ear	6
back	32
thigh	25
thumb	21
stomach	18
mouth	8
head	1
ankle	29
hip	23
eyebrow	3
elbow	15
neck	31
waist	17
chin	9
throat	11
finger	22
shoulder	32
arm	14
breast	16
foot	30
wrist	19
armpit	13
groin	24
calf	27
bottom	34
eye	4
jaw	10
nose	5

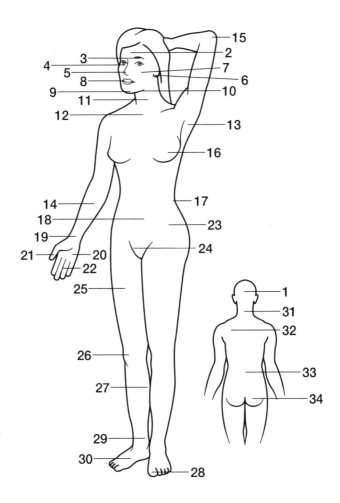

Patients don't use medical terminology but rather
use these common words to describe parts of
the body. It is important to know them. Children
will sometimes use different words, for example
tummy instead of *stomach*.

2 Body systems

Which body system are the following medical terms connected with?

1. movement, bone, cartilage, ribs
   S K E L E T A L   S Y S T E M

2. ova, menstruation, semen, oestrogen
   R _ _ _ _ _ _ _ _ _ _   S Y S T E M

3. hair, sweat, verruca, pustules
   I _ _ _ _ _ _ _ _ _ _ _   S Y S T E M

4. thyroid, carriers, gland, neurosecretion
   E _ _ _ _ _ _ _ _   S Y S T E M

5. vein, valve, pressure, aorta
   C _ _ _ _ _ _ _ _ _ _ _ R   S Y S T E M

6. peritoneal cavity, chewing, absorption, villi
   D _ _ _ _ _ _ _ E   S Y S T E M

7. urea, bladder, cortex, nephron
   U _ _ _ _ _ _   S Y S T E M

8. striated, contraction, fibres, tendon
   S _ _ _ _ _ _   M _ _ _ _ _ S

9. leucocytes, coagulation, anaemia, fibrin
   H _ _ _ _ _ _ _ _ _ _

10. vessels, nodes, marrow, infection
    L _ _ _ _ _ _ _ _   S Y S T E M

11. neurones, sensitivity, brain, olfactory
    N _ _ _ _ _ _   S Y S T E M

12. bronchus, mucus, nose, ventilation
    R _ _ _ _ _ _ _ _ Y   S Y S T E M

- You may only know two or three words in the sets above, but that should be enough to identify the system.
- Words spelt with *oe* or *ae* in British English (*oestrogen*, *anaemia*) take *e* only in American English spelling (*estrogen*, *anemia*).

3 Basic terms

Match the definitions with the terms. Write the letters in the grid below.

1	the long-term results of an illness or treatment	a	disease
2	identifying several illnesses which the patient may have	b	symptoms
3	things wrong with the body which the patient complains of or experiences	c	history
4	a study of the patient's body	d	examination
5	the causes leading to an illness	e	prevention
6	an unusual feature which may be worrying or dangerous	f	consultation
7	a meeting between patient and doctor to discuss problems	g	abnormality
8	the identification of a particular illness	h	sequelae
9	a change in the structure or function of the organs or tissue of the body	i	aetiology
10	taking away the cause of illness or finding it early	j	complications
11	a group of signs which are characteristic of a particular illness	k	prognosis
12	additional problems to the original illness	l	signs
13	likely outcome of an illness	m	syndrome
14	a patient's medical background, problems, behaviour and lifestyle	n	differential diagnosis
15	what the doctor can see of the illness	o	diagnosis

1	2	3	4	5	6	7	8	9	10	11	12	13	14	15
h														

4 Word roots

Match up the roots with the part of the body. Notice that some parts of the body use two or three roots.

aur-	~~brachi-~~	bucca-	capit-	carp-	cephal-	cervic-
cheir-	corpor-	dactyl-	digit-	faci-	mamm-	man-
mast-	nas-	ocul-	ophthalm-	or-	ot-	pect-	ped-
pod-	rhin-	somat-	steth-	stom(at)-	thorac-	trachel-

arm   _brachi-_

body   _____   _____

breast   _____   _____

cheek   _____

chest   _____   _____   _____

ear   _____   _____

eye   _____   _____

face   _____

finger/toe   _____   _____

foot   _____   _____

hand   _____   _____

head   _____   _____

mouth   _____   _____

neck   _____   _____

nose   _____   _____

wrist   _____

About 75% of medical terms come from Greek or Latin. The root forms the basis of the word. _Cervix-_ is often used for the narrow part of an organ; _stoma-_ is used for an opening onto a surface. Examples of words built on all of the above roots are given in the answer section. Try to think of some on your own first. See also: Test 43.

5 Basic hospital vocabulary

Rearrange the letters in brackets to form the correct word.

1 People in hospital with some form of illness are known as _*patients*_ .
(ptientas)

2 When they first arrive at hospital, a doctor or nurse _____ them
and shows them to a bed in a _____ . (tdamis) (draw)

3 There may be a letter of _____ from another doctor explaining
the history. (learrfer)

4 The doctor may have to complete a _____ for tests. (sequert)

5 Many medical personnel have to be ready to go to work in the event of
an emergency if they are _____-_____ . (cloanl)

6 The doctor may decide to have blood, urine or tissue _____
analysed. (sencemips)

7 Every day the doctor will speak to the patients during the _____
_____ . (draw undor)

8 Patients who require surgery will be asked to sign a _____ form.
(steconn)

9 A patient who is well enough to go home will be _____ .
(chagisdred)

10 A patient who does not need to stay in hospital overnight can see the
hospital specialist as an _____ and will be given an appointment
to attend the _____ . (pattitoune) (liccin)

11 When colleagues are absent from work because of illness, others will
have to _____ . (crove)

12 Patients who are getting better are _____ . (stealnecconv)

13 The hospital may arrange for a _____ when doctors are on
holiday. (cloum)

A team of doctors working together in a hospital is known as a **firm**. A firm
may have patients on different wards, but on one particular ward there may
be patients from different firms.

6 Basic pathology

Complete the spider diagram with the following words.

| asthma | ~~biopsy~~ | cyanide | environment | infections | manifestations |
| neoplastic | pathogenesis | physical | starvation | ultrasound |

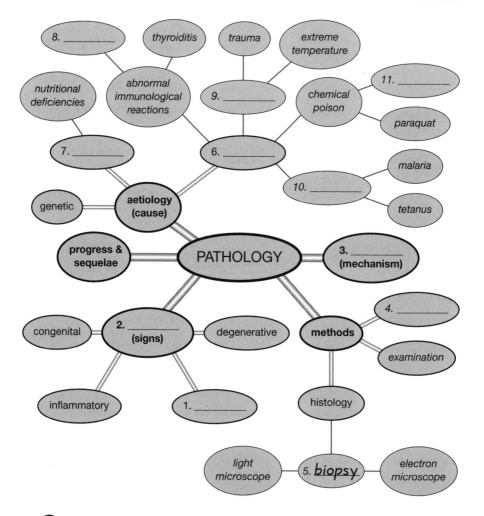

8. _____ thyroiditis trauma extreme temperature

nutritional deficiencies abnormal immunological reactions 9. _____ chemical poison 11. _____

paraquat

7. _____ 6. _____

malaria

10. _____

genetic aetiology (cause) tetanus

progress & sequelae PATHOLOGY 3. _____ (mechanism)

4. _____

congenital 2. _____ (signs) degenerative methods

examination

inflammatory 1. _____ histology

light microscope 5. *biopsy* electron microscope

Using a spider diagram is one way to organize vocabulary. As you learn new vocabulary you can add to the diagram. You can also begin new spiders for subsections of the original diagram. You can copy out parts of the diagram above and add words you know now and add more words in the future.

7 Describing symptoms

What do the following adjectives describe? Complete the sentences below.
Choose from the following.

anxious	barking	bitter	~~blurry~~	confused	creamy
double	faint	foul	hawking	husky	light	nauseating
numb	offensive	pinkish	pounding	salty	slimy	sour
stiff	stinky	sweet	tense	throbbing	tingling
transparent	unclear	weak	wheezing	woozy

1 My sight is ___*blurry*___ , _____ , _____ .

2 I feel _____ , _____ , _____ ,
_____ .

3 My headache is _____ , _____ , _____ ,
_____ .

4 My leg feels _____ , _____ , _____ ,
_____ .

5 His cough sounds _____ , _____ ,
_____ , _____ .

6 Food tastes _____ , _____ , _____ ,
_____ .

7 The discharge smells _____ , _____ ,
_____ , _____ .

8 The discharge is _____ , _____ , _____ ,
_____ .

Many common adjectives are formed by adding -y to the noun or -ing to the
verb. The suffix -ish means 'sort of' or 'a bit' and is used mainly with shapes
and colours (e.g. roundish, pinkish). Patients may use these adjectives but
they are very imprecise and you may need to ask for clarification. See also:
Test 10.

8 Shape

A Complete the following tables.

Two-dimensional shapes	Noun	Adjective
	square	square
	circle	_____
	triangle	_____
	_____	semicircular
	_____	_____-shaped

Three-dimensional shapes	Noun	Adjective
	_____	spherical
	hemisphere	_____
	cylinder	_____
	cone	_____
	_____	pyramidal

B Describe the shape of the following. The first two have been done for you.

_____pear_____ -shaped   _____ -shaped   _____ -shaped

_____ -shaped   _____ -shaped   _____ -shaped

_____ -shaped   _____ -shaped   _____ -shaped

_____ -shaped   _____ -shaped   _____ -shaped

C Match up the shape with the part of the body.

funnel-shaped ———————— bars of cartilage in the trachea
pear-shaped   hyoid bone
dome-shaped   orbit
tubular   atlas (1st vertebra)
hoop-shaped   sacrum and coccyx
tapering wedge-shaped   femur
horseshoe-shaped   diaphragm
pyramidal   uterus
C-shaped   infundibulum (fallopian tubes)

Anatomical descriptions normally include a description of shape. There is a large number of possible shape descriptions as in C above. Many shapes are described as letter-shaped (*A-shaped* etc.) or as easily recognized object shapes (*star-shaped*, *kidney-shaped* etc.). You will no doubt meet more shapes when reading.

9 Bones and joints 1

Fill in the crossword.

Across

1   A bone in the arm which sounds as though it should be funny!

4   The last bone in the back.

7   A little bone in the throat.

9   The patient calls this the collar bone.

11   This bone in the ear means 'anvil'.

12   Another word for lower jaw.

13   It protects the brain.

17   The final limb bones.

20   It provides support, movement and protection.

21   The patient calls this the funny bone!

22   This is known as the knee cap.

23   This is the spherical top end of the femur.

24   Arms and legs.

26   Joints allow bones to do this.

27   The shin bone.

28   You will find the metatarsals here.

Down

2   One of the bones in the lower arm.

3   There's fluid in this type of joint.

5   The socket for the eye.

6   The most abundant extracellular fibre in the body!

8   The common name for spinal column.

10   These protect vital body organs.

14 It's tough, flexible and much lighter than bone.

15 This is one of the bones forming the spinal column.

16 These attach muscle to bone.

18 Commonly called the breast bone.

19 A small pit in the cartilage on the femur.

25 The long central section of the femur.

 The five fingers on the hand are called: **thumb**, **index**, **middle**, **ring** and **little finger**.

10 Bones and joints 2: word building 1

Use the word in capitals to form an adjective in each of the following.

1   The bones in the body form the ___*skeletal*___
    system.   SKELETON

2   Tendons connecting muscle to bone are _____ ,
    allowing the body to move.   FLEX

3   Bone is more _____ than cartilage.   RESIST

4   The skull consists of the _____   CRANIUM,
    and _____ skeleton.   FACE

5   The bone surrounds a _____ blood vessel.   CENTRE

6   Spicules of bone are surrounded by _____
    tissue.   CONNECT

7   A bone has a tough _____ outer membrane. COLLAGEN

8   The hollow _____ shape of the femur resists
    stress.   TUBE

9   Some bones have a _____ function.   PROTECT

10 The joints between vertebrae are _____ joints.
                                                                     CARTILAGE

11 The elbow, hip and wrist are _____ joints.   MOVE

12 In a synovial joint there is a _____ fluid
    between the surfaces.   LUBRICATE

13 _____ contraction changes the length of
    the muscle.   MUSCLE

14 The ligaments connecting the tarsus bones are very
    _____ .   POWER

15 The spinal column is also known as the
    _____ column.   VERTEBRA

The adjectives above are formed with different suffixes: -al, -ible, -ant, -ive,
-ous, -ar, -ful, -ing. Try to think of some more adjectives which end in these
suffixes before you look at examples given in the answer section. See also:
Test 7.

11 The heart

Fill in the missing words in the sentences below. Choose from the following.

> arteries   arterioles   atria   beats   branch   capillaries   cavity
> chambers   circulatory   close   communicate   contraction   cusps
> heart   lungs   ~~muscle~~   oxygenated   pulse   pump   pumping
> pyramidal   relaxation   systemic   valves   veins   vessels   wall   wrist

1 Many people feel the most important _muscle_ in the body is the heart. Together with the _____ system it maintains life. The heart is roughly _____ in shape and is located in the pericardial _____ .

2 The heart is divided into right and left halves which do not _____ .

3 Blood travels round the body in blood _____ . The _____ carry blood from the heart to all parts of the body while blood returns to the heart in _____ .

4 The pulmonary artery carries blood from the heart to the _____ , while the aorta carries blood to all parts of the body from the _____ .

5 Blood carried in the systemic arteries is _____ but in the pulmonary artery it is not.

6 The heart is a _____ with four _____ , two ventricles and two _____ . The left ventricle has a much thicker _____ than the right because it is responsible for _____ blood around the _____ circulatory system. Blood is forced round the system by _____ (systole) and _____ (diastole) of the heart.

7 The pulmonary and aortic _____ control the exits from the ventricles. Each one has three _____ . The sound of the heart is when they _____ .

8 Each minute the heart _____ about 72 times. This is known as the _____ rate and can be measured in the radial artery in the _____ .

9 The systemic arteries _____ (divide) many times and become _____ . They then deliver blood to small _____ from where exchange can take place.

12 The digestive system

A   Match the common term on the left with the medical term on the right.

mouth	oesophagus
roof of the mouth	duodenum, jejunum, ileum, colon, and rectum
spit	buccal cavity
throat	colon
gullet	saliva
small intestine	hard and soft palate
large intestine	pharynx
bowel	ileum

B   Label the diagram.

duodenum	_____
large intestine	_____
salivary gland	_____
gullet	_____
rectum	_____
stomach	_____
pancreas	_____
appendix	_____
gall bladder	_____
caecum	_____
mouth	_____
liver	_____
small intestine	_____
roof of the mouth	_____
anus	_____
tongue	_____
bile duct	_____
throat	_____

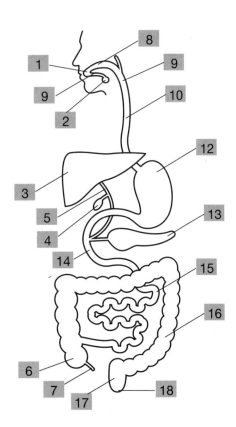

13 The respiratory system

Match up the beginning of sentences 1–15 with the appropriate ending a–o to form fifteen true sentences about respiration.

1 External respiration involves taking oxygen into the body and

2 From the nose and mouth, air flows

3 The trachea divides

4 Gaseous exchange takes place

5 Ventilation is the process of

6 The respiratory tract is lined with

7 The mucus in the respiratory tract is continually moved

8 Residual air is left behind in the lungs

9 During heavy exercise, the depth and rate of ventilation

10 The epiglottis prevents

11 The larynx is also known as

12 Each of the two lungs is surrounded

13 The pleural cavities are filled

14 Air flows into the lungs when

15 Tensing the vocal folds in the larynx in a stream of air

a by cilia.

b food and liquid from entering the lower respiratory tract.

c renewing alveolar air.

d causes them to vibrate and produce sound.

e increases dramatically.

f by its pleural cavity.

g into the larynx and windpipe.

h the chest wall and diaphragm move to increase the volume of the thorax.

i getting rid of excess carbon dioxide.

j with fluid.

k in the alveoli.

l after expiration.

m into the right and left bronchi.

n the voice box or Adam's apple.

o a layer of sticky mucus.

14 The nervous system

Rearrange the letters in brackets to form the correct word.

1 The brain and spinal cord form the ___central___ nervous system (CNS). (calnetr)

2 The nerves which connect the brain and structures of the head are _____ nerves. (cnalira)

3 An immediate response of the body to a stimulus is a _____ action. (rxfele)

4 Messages are transmitted along nerve fibres by means of action _____ . (pnialteto)

5 A stimulus is received by a _____ . (rtreecpo)

6 The muscle or gland which responds to a stimulus is the _____ . (etorfecf)

7 Nerve cells are known as _____ . (nnurseeo)

8 Nerve fibres are connected by a junction or _____ . (spsenay)

9 At these junctions, signalling molecules or _____ are released. (netrmituoanstersr)

10 Normally nerve cells are divided into three types: _____ , motor and _____ . (synesor), (aumoustnoo)

11 A motor cell consists of a cell body with _____ protruding from it and a long _____ . (ddsteiner) (oaxn)

12 In the spinal cord, neuronal cell bodies are known as _____ . (rgye teramt)

13 Nerves which supply the body wall, skeletal muscle and skin are _____ nerves. (sctmoai)

14 A collection of neuronal cell bodies lying outside the CNS is called a _____ . (gnoaling)

15 The internal environment of the body is controlled by the _____ nervous system. (amtiuotca)

16 'Fight, fright or flight' is controlled by the _____ nervous system. (scmythpaeit)

Impulse is a common term which may be used for action potential.

15 Embryo to birth

Choose an adjective and a noun to complete the sentences below.

Adjectives	Nouns
amniotic, birth, breech, dilated, ~~fallopian~~, foetal, lanugo, maternal, menstrual, multiple, premature, umbilical, uterine	baby, blood, canal, cervix, contractions, cord, fluid, hair, monitoring, period, position, pregnancy, ~~tubes~~

1   Fertilization takes place in the _fallopian_ _tubes_ .
2   The foetus develops within a sac containing _____ _____ to protect against injury.
3   Oxygen and nutrients are obtained from _____ _____ through the placenta.
4   At sixteen weeks the foetus is covered in fine _____ _____ .
5   Vernix eases the baby's passage down the _____ _____ .
6   Pregnancy normally lasts forty weeks from the first day of a woman's last _____ _____ .
7   During labour, _____ _____ become stronger and more regular.
8   Having more than one foetus in the womb is known as a _____ _____ .
9   A fully _____ _____ has an opening of about 10 cm.
10 A _____ _____ is when the baby is lying head upwards before delivery.
11 _____ _____ allows the midwife to check the unborn baby's heart rate during labour.
12 After the baby has been born the midwife clamps the _____ _____ in two places.
13 A _____ _____ will often be placed in an incubator.

Many words are used in association with other words to form collocations, e.g. *premature baby*, *birth canal*. Try to learn these words in these partnerships. This will help you when reading and listening. In Test 54 you can practise more collocations.

16 The urinary system

Fill in the missing verbs in the following text. Choose from the following but you will have to change them into the simple present passive voice.

absorb	alter	call	eliminate	feel	form	lose
pump	recover	reflect	retain	separate		set up
	situate	store	surround	transport		

In the urinary system, waste (1) __is eliminated__ by the kidneys. A filtrate of water, ion and small molecules (2) _____ from the blood which comes from the renal artery.

The kidney consists of about 1 million units which (3) _____ nephrons. Each nephron is a complicated structure positioned partly in the medulla and partly in the cortex of the kidney.

The glomeruli and proximal convoluted tubules (4) _____ in the renal cortex. The glomerulus is a coiled mass of capillaries which (5) _____ by specialized cells. Fluid leaves the capillaries and passes into the lumen of the nephron. The electrolyte composition of the blood (6) _____ in the urinary filtrate. Plasma proteins and blood cells do not pass out but (7) _____ in the capillaries.

In the proximal convoluted tubule, sodium ions (8) _____ back into the body. Sugars and amino acids (9) _____ from the filtrate and most of the water (10) _____ by the end of the proximal convoluted tubule.

In the loop of Henle, the composition of the filtrate
(11) _____ hardly _____ but a gradient of
sodium concentration (12) _____ .

Water and ions are further recovered in the distal convoluted tubule.
Collecting ducts (13) _____ by several distal convoluted
tubules. In the collecting ducts, ions and small molecules such as urea
are retained but water (14) _____ to the surroundings.

Urine (15) _____ in the ureters from each kidney to the
bladder where it (16) _____ . When the volume of urine
reaches between 200 and 300 ml a desire to void urine
(17) _____ . Urine is conveyed from the bladder to the
exterior via the urethra.

The passive voice is used to describe processes like those above. It is
formed with the verb *be* and the past participle of the main verb. Regular
verbs simply add *-d* or *-ed* but you must learn irregular verbs. Luckily, most
scientific verbs are regular, but there are three irregular verbs above.

17 The reproductive system

Use the clues to fill in the missing letters in the following terms below.

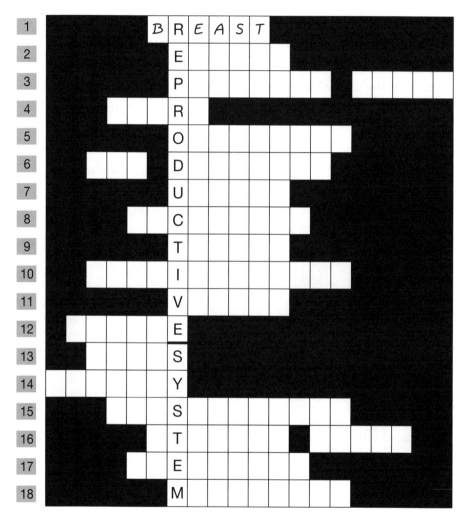

#							
1	B	R	E	A	S	T	
2			E				
3			P				
4			R				
5			O				
6			D				
7			U				
8			C				
9			T				
10			I				
11			V				
12			E				
13			S				
14			Y				
15			S				
16			T				
17			E				
18			M				

1   After birth, secretions from this feed the baby.

2   A tiny mass of cells which grows in the wall of the uterus.

3   This produces the greater part of the semen.

4   One of a pair where female germ cells are produced.

5   The expulsion of a mature oocyte into the peritoneal cavity.

6   One of a pair of tubes which carry sperm.

7   The chamber where a new individual develops.

8   The production of milk.

9   Lying in the scrotum, they produce sperm.

10   The result of this is a zygote.

11   The channel through which a baby is born.

12   It lies at the centre of the areola.

13   It is erectile during copulation.

14   The time when teenagers become sexually mature.

15   The breakdown and expulsion of the lining of the uterus once a month.

16   Fertilization takes place here.

17   The period of nine months during which a new individual develops.

18   When the menstrual cycle ceases in women of 45–55 years of age.

18 The skin

A   Label the diagram.

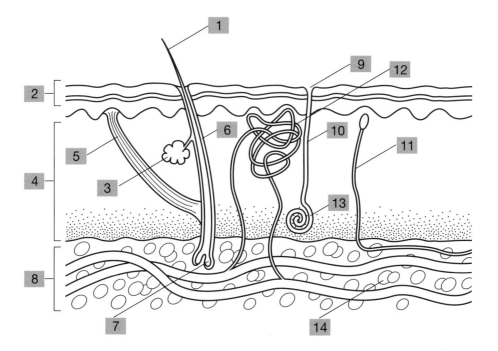

hair	_____	blood capillaries	_____
epidermis	_____	pore	_____
subcutaneous fat	_____	hair bulb	_____
nerve fibre	_____	sweat gland	_____
sebaceous gland	_____	duct	_____
arrector muscle	_____	hypodermis	_____
dermis	_____	hair follicle	_____

B Now match mechanism a–k with function 1–10. One function has three mechanisms.

	Function		**Mechanism**
1	protection against water loss	a	collagen and elastin in the dermis
2	protection against micro-organisms	b	conversion of subcutaneous fat
3	screen from UV rays	c	erection of hairs
4	shield against mechanical abrasion	d	greasy horny layer
5	monitoring of the environment	e	nerve endings in the dermis
6	formation of vitamin D	f	epidermal melanin
7	temperature regulation	g	sweat production
8	energy storage	h	evaporation of sweat
9	excretion of mainly salt and water	i	increased cell division and replacement
10	protection against stretching	j	synthesis from 7-dehydrocholesterol
		k	compounds from sweat and sebaceous glands
		l	control of dermal blood flow

19 Hormones

Replace the words in brackets with a more medical term. Choose from the following.

> accelerates consequences continuous bind buffer derive disequilibrium
> excite fluctuate inhibit intermittent maintains metabolism
> overproduction regulator ~~secreted~~ stimulate underproduction

1 The endocrine system operates by a system of hormones which are (produced) __secreted__ into the blood stream.

2 Hormones either (increase) _____ or (slow) _____ the activity of specific cells.

3 Many hormones (join) _____ to carrier proteins and this has a (protective) _____ effect against sudden changes.

4 Hormone levels generally (go up and down) _____ but within limits. The production of thyroxine is (all the time) _____ while the production of other hormones is (from time to time) _____ .

5 Any (imbalance) _____ in the endocrine system can have important (results) _____ . Problems in the endocrine system usually involve (making too much) _____ or (making too little) _____ .

6 Growth hormone is important in children to (encourage) _____ growth.

7 The adrenal glands (get) _____ some of their blood supply from the renal artery.

8 Calcitonin and parathormone are involved in the (utilization) _____ of calcium. Parathormone (keeps) _____ plasma calcium levels within normal limits.

9 Aldosterone is the most important (controller) _____ of sodium and potassium. Thyroxine (speeds up) _____ the release of energy in the tissues.

> The prefixes used in the answers above have particular meanings. *over-* = too much; *under-* = not enough, *inter-* = between ; *dis-* = not. You will meet these prefixes regularly so it's good to understand their meaning. See also: Test 50.

20 The eye and the ear

Choose the correct answer.

1 When a patient refers to the white of the eye he means

a) the sclera   b) the lens   c) the cornea   d) the fovea

2 The lacrimal gland produces

a) lactase   b) tears   c) mucus   d) spit

3 The yellow spot is

a) the pupil   b) the choroids
c) the fovea   d) the optic nerve

4 The eye photoreceptors are

a) rods and cones   b) optic nerve
c) iris   d) visual cortex

5 To blink is to

a) respond to dim light   b) to lower the eyelid
c) to contract the lateral rectus   d) to activate the lacrimal glands

6 The ear drum is

a) the auricle   b) the tympanic membrane
c) the cochlea   d) fenestra vestibuli

7 The stirrup is

a) malleus   b) incus   c) stapes   d) saccule

8 The ear lobe is the

a) pinna   b) ossicles
c) cochlea   d) fenestra cochleae

9 The round window is the

a) fenestra cochleae   b) fenestra vestibuli
c) malleus   d) semicircular canal

10 The Eustachian tube allows our ears to

a) pop   b) drain   c) bang   d) close

11 Cerumen is known as

a) fluid   b) hairs   c) paste   d) wax

21 Taking a history

Put the following questions in the dialogue below.

a   And since that incident?

b   Now, can you tell me about your lifestyle? Do you smoke or drink?

c   Have you experienced any problems in your legs at all?

d   What's the problem with your chest?

e   Can you describe this pain?

f   What seems to be the trouble?

g   And how long did the pain last?

h   Do you think the weather affects it?

i   And what about your family? Is there any history of heart problems or blood pressure problems?

j   I see, and how is business at the moment?

k   Can you tell me a bit more about these pains?

l   Have you got a job?

1   Good morning Mr Lin. My name's Dr Frank. *What seems to be the trouble?*

It's my chest, doctor.

2   _____

Well, I sometimes get pains in it.

3   I see. _____

Well it started when I was on holiday and I had to climb a steep hill from the town to our hotel. I got a bad pain in my chest.

4   _____

It was across the front of my chest and sort of up into my neck. My arms felt heavy and I couldn't get my breath.

5 _____

Only a few minutes and then I was OK again.

6 _____

I've felt it several times recently, usually when I'm lifting things or rushing. I just can't get my breath.

7 _____

Yes, on cold days it's worse.

8 _____

I smoke the occasional cigar and I like a dram in the evening. But I'm not a heavy drinker!

9 Of course not! _____

I have my own business. A small printing company.

10 _____

Not very good, actually. There's too much competition from the big companies.

11 Mm! _____

_____

No, not that I know of.

12 _____

No, I haven't.

OK. Thank you Mr Lin. Now I'd like to examine you if you don't mind.

It's important to use open questions as much as possible when interviewing patients to allow them to offer and explain as much as they feel able to. While the patient is speaking it is often possible to pick up on clues about contributing factors. For this you need good listening skills.

22 Family and social history

Match the question with the answer.

1	Can I ask how old you are?	**a**	I cycle to work normally.
2	How long have you been married?	**b**	About twenty a day.
3	What form of contraception do you use?	**c**	I'm not sure, just old age I think!
4	Do you take any exercise?	**d**	My husband uses a condom.
5	Have you ever had an X-ray of your chest?	**e**	Yes, I worked in East Africa for two years.
6	Can I ask you about your parents?	**f**	I'm fifty-five.
7	What did your father die from?	**g**	When I was fifteen, I think.
8	Have you ever lived in a tropical country?	**h**	Yes, but it was a long time ago.
9	Is there anything which is worrying you at the moment?	**i**	One or two glasses of wine each day.
10	What do you do?	**j**	I work in a clothing factory.
11	How many cigarettes do you smoke?	**k**	I think I only had measles.
12	How much do you drink?	**l**	Twenty-five years. It's our silver wedding this year!
13	When did your periods first begin?	**m**	They're both dead now.
14	Which childhood illnesses did you have?	**n**	Nothing more than the usual daily problems.

When asking for facts it is normally acceptable to use short closed questions (*Do you..*, *When..*, *How many..*, *What..*). However, if you are asking about something fairly personal or sensitive it is necessary to use a polite question form such as: *Can I ask ....?* or *Can/could you tell me about ....?*

23 Polite requests

Correct the mistake in each of the following.

1   Let's having a look at you!

2   Could you just turn over your body, please?

3   I'd like you walk slowly across the room.

4   Can you reading the first letter on the board?

5   Would you just to stand on the scales, please?

6   Now try to press just a little bit hard.

7   I wondering if you could show me your tummy?

8   Do you like to just slip off your socks and shoes?

9   Would you mind wait outside for a few moments?

10 Try hard staying as still as possible!

11 So, you can putting your things back on now!

12 Please tell me if you would feel any discomfort.

13 Do you think you would lie on your left side, please?

14 Could you find possibly someone to bring you to the clinic next week?

 Notice that the verb in *I was wondering* is in the past tense although the meaning is not past! There is a small difference between *would* and *could*; *would* introduces a polite instruction while *could* introduces a polite request. See also: Test 60.

24 Giving instructions

Fill in the missing words in the following instructions. Choose from the box.

bend	~~clench~~	close	cough	grip	hold	lie	lift	open	read
relax	rest	roll	say	show	stand	stretch	take	touch	turn

1   Can you _clench_ your fist?

2   _____ me your hands, please

3   Could you _____ your mouth?

4   Just _____ your arm, please.

5   _____ a deep breath.

6   _____ Aaaah!

7   _____ the bar tightly!

8   Can you _____ the letters?

9   _____ , please.

10   Can you _____ your leg?

11   _____ as far as you can!

12   Can you _____ your toes?

13   Can you try to _____ on one leg?

14   Can you _____ over, please?

15   You can _____ your mouth now!

16   Could you _____ down, please?

17   And _____ your breath!

18   Just _____ up your sleeve, please!

19   Can you _____ your arm here?

20   Don't worry! _____ !

- It is considered impolite in English to issue instructions as commands, e.g. '**Roll up** your sleeve!' '**Sit down!**' It's much more acceptable to form requests with can or could. You can also reduce the impact of a command by beginning with just e.g. 'Just sit down please'. And of course don't forget to use Please!

- **Can** may also be used when asking about a person's ability to do something, e.g. Can you move your leg (or is it too painful)?

25 Articles of clothing

Label the clothes. Choose from the following.

socks	_9_	nightdress	____	pocket	____
cardigan	____	knickers	____	sleeve	____
vest	____	tie	____	skirt	____
jacket	____	hat	____	scarf	____
boots	____	laces	____	zip	____
trousers	____	collar	____	button	____
bra	____	jumper	____	cuff	____
underpants	____	shirt	____	dressing gown	____
pyjamas	____	top	____		

 Lady's *knickers* are also called *pants* or *briefs*. A man wears a *shirt* but a woman wears a *blouse*. Matching jacket and trousers/skirt are a *suit*. A *nightdress* is often abbreviated to *nightie*, especially by children.

26 Abbreviations

What do the following abbreviations stand for?

A3	_____
AF	_____
A/G ratio	_____
AS	_____
BOR	_____
BP	_____
° ↑ BP	_____
Cgh	_____
CO	_____
C/O	_____
CVS	_____
D&C	_____
DM	_____
DOB	_____
DVT	_____
Ep	_____
G and A	_____
HPC	_____
° JACCOL	_____
LBP	_____
° LKKS	_____
MI	_____
MRU	_____
N&V	_____
OD	_____
O/E	_____
OPA	_____
PM	_____
PMH	_____
PR	_____
RS	_____
Sat	_____
SH	_____
SOB	_____
T	_____
° TB	_____
U/S	_____
XR	_____

° indicates no/not present/not detected; ↑ indicates raised/increased.

 There are numerous abbreviations used in the medical profession but they may vary from one speciality to another or from person to person. To avoid any potential misunderstandings, vital information should be written out in full.

27 Common complaints

Complete the following complaints. Choose from the following.

black eye	bruise	can't sleep	~~cough~~	depressed
headache	insect bite	lost my appetite	lump	nosebleed
out of breath	runny nose	sore throat		stomach-ache
	swollen leg	temperature		

1 I've got a

_____cough_____ and

a _____ .

2 When I climb the stairs I'm _____ .

3 I don't want to eat; I've _____ .

4 At night time I go to bed but I _____ .

5 I've got a

_____

and a

_____

.

6   I knocked my arm on the door and now I've got a big

_____ .

7   I got an

_____

two days ago and

now I've got a

_____ .

8   I fell down the stairs and now

I've got a _____

and a _____ .

9   I feel so miserable. I'm really

_____ .

10   I'm a bit worried because I

can feel a _____

in my breast.

11   I regularly get a

_____ .

12   After I eat I regularly

get a _____ .

28 Understanding the patient

When a patient says the following, what does he/she mean? Circle the letter of the correct answer.

1 My last doctor *put me on* antibiotics.
a) withdrew
b) prescribed
c) replaced
d) recommended

2 I've *blacked out* three times in the last week.
a) defaecated
b) vomited
c) suffered neuralgia
d) fainted

3 The rash on my skin seems to have *cleared up.*
a) become infected
b) spread
c) disappeared
d) got worse

4 I often *nod off* for just a few minutes.
a) fall asleep
b) feel nauseous
c) have a hot flush
d) feel tired

5 My sister *passed away* recently.
a) developed cancer
b) had an operation
c) had a leg amputated
d) died

6 I don't seem to be able to *take* anything *in.*
a) eat
b) drink
c) understand
d) feel

7 I sometimes *bring up* my food.
a) swallow
b) regurgitate
c) cut up into small pieces
d) have no appetite for

8 I walk to town and back and then I'm *flaked out.*
a) cold
b) suffering pain
c) exhausted
d) breathless

9 She *threw up* several times during the night.
a) woke up
b) defaecated
c) experienced pain
d) vomited

10 My eye is all *puffed up.*
a) swollen
b) unable to see clearly
c) discoloured
d) itching

29 Places in the hospital

Where would you find the following in a hospital? Fill in the missing letters.

1. all medical files, letters, and reports

    M E D I C A L R E C O R D S

2. women having babies

    _ A B O U _   _ A R _

3. someone having an operation

    _ H E A T R _

4. specimens being analysed

    _ A B O R A T O R _

5. patients who have just finished undergoing surgery

    _ E C O V E R _   _ R E _

6. people moving between rooms and departments

    _ O R R I D O _

7. staff and visitors eating

    _ A N T E E _

8. people that have recently died

    _ O R T U A R _

9. seriously ill people receiving specialist nursing

    _ N T E N S I V _   _ A R _

10. patients from accidents and disasters

    _ C C I D E N _ & _ M E R G E N C _

11. drugs being dispensed

    _ H A R M A C _

12. stored blood

    _ L O O _   _ A N _

13. people who have had a heart attack

    _ O R O N A R _   _ A R _   _ N I _

14. patients being moved between floors

    _ I F _

15. elderly patients

    _ E R I A T R I _   _ A R _

30 People in the hospital

Match up the person with the correct definition and write your answers in the box.

1 They assist patients who have difficulties speaking.

2 They move patients on beds, trolleys and wheelchairs.

3 They look after people's feet.

4 They work out special meals and give advice on the most appropriate food.

5 They are responsible for, prepare and dispense medicine.

6 These doctors' speciality is children.

7 Senior medical people who give expert advice and are responsible for final decision making.

8 They give massage and exercise to restore specific bodily functions.

9 They operate on patients to repair skin damage or improve a patient's appearance.

10 Their work is rehabilitation and assistance of people recovering from or suffering from illness.

11 They operate equipment in the X-ray department.

12 They work in the departments which are responsible for specimens.

13 They are responsible for running and organizing a ward or department.

14 They work together with medical personnel in hospital and try to deal with a patient's problems at home.

15 They clean and organize bed linen.

16 These doctors may refer their patients to hospital to see a specialist or to receive specialist care.

a	consultants
b	physiotherapists
c	ward sisters/charge nurses
d	plastic surgeons
e	speech therapists
f	chiropodists
g	social workers
h	medical laboratory scientific officers
i	radiographers
j	dieticians
k	porters
l	pharmacists
m	laundry staff
n	general practitioners
o	paediatricians
p	occupational therapists

1	2	3	4	5	6	7	8	9	10	11	12	13	14	15	16
e															

Senior surgeons and consultants who are Fellows of the Royal College of Surgeons (FRCS) use the title *Mr* in Britain. Other doctors use the title *Dr.* Nurses have different qualifications and the hierarchy is *Staff nurses, Enrolled nurses, Student nurses, Auxiliary nurses.*

31 Letter of referral

There are two letters below. One is a letter of referral from a general practitioner to a consultant and the other the consultant's reply. Fill in the missing words. Choose from the following.

discomfort	drip	examination	findings	~~grateful~~
instance	nasal	obstruction	opinion	persist
persistently	respond	responds	response	

Consultant: Mr Holger Bauer
Patient name: John Gardner
DOB: 14/07/80
07/05/02

Dear Mr Bauer
I would be (1) ___*grateful*___ if you could see this young man who has had a (2) _____ blocked nose over the last few months. On two occasions I have noted polyps. They
(3) _____ to a small degree to beclamethasone
(4) _____ spray, but continue to (5) _____ .
I would be grateful for your (6) _____ .

Yours sincerely

Ivan Nazareva

Ivan Nazarova (Dr)

Department of Otolaryngology
New patient consultation: John Gardner, DOB 14/07/80
25/06/02   (Clinic 19/06/02)

Dear Dr Nazarova

Thank you for asking me to see this 21-year-old telecommunications engineer.

Presentation and (7) _____ :
He complains of long-standing nasal (8) _____ on both sides with only partial (9) _____ to Beconase nasal spray. He also says that his ears pop occasionally and he gets some facial (10) _____ and post nasal (11) _____ .

On (12) _____ today his nose showed congested nasal mucosa and polypoid middle turbinate and small middle meatal polyps.

Impression and plan:
In the first (13) _____ , I have started him on a course of Nasonex nasal spray which is a more modern steroid spray than Beconase. I shall see him again in two months' time to see how he (14) _____ .

Yours sincerely

Holger Bauer

Holger Bauer

Consultant Otolaryngologist

Notice that only widely recognized abbreviations are used in these sorts of letters. In order to avoid misunderstandings, it is best to write them in full.

32 Confusing words

Choose the correct word in each of the following.

1 She nervously waited for the post to find out whether she had *past/passed* her final nursing examination.

2 He seems to have put on a lot of *weight/wait* in the last few months.

3 A new *sight/site* on the edge of the city has now been found for the new hospital.

4 One quality that all nurses must have is *patience/patients*.

5 She is very concerned that her hair loss will result in her becoming *balled/bald*.

6 During the procedure she began to feel unwell and felt she was going to *feint/faint*.

7 He has been experiencing pain in the *lumbar/lumber* region of the back.

8 The surgeon uses a large number of *slobs/swabs* to mop up the blood.

9 Muscular dystrophy is a disease where the muscles *waist/waste* away.

10 He suffers from a muscular *tic/tick* in his left eye.

11 In the accident he suffered a major *break/brake* to his right femur.

12 After sneezing or coughing, some microbial pathogens may be *born/borne* on the wind, enhancing the spread of infection.

13 Before going off duty the doctor should *cheque/check* that all intravenous cannulae are working satisfactorily.

14 The wound has been very slow to *heel/heal*.

15 The doctor was called when the child began to *grown/groan* with pain.

16 Her skin was badly *pitted/pitied* with the scars of acne.

17 As the infection took hold his temperature began to *soar/sore*.

 Most of the potentially confusing words above present a spelling problem. You may need a good English dictionary to help you. Look up the wrong words too to see what someone may have unintentionally said!

33 Procedures

The following phrases are spoken by a nurse carrying out nasogastric intubation. They are all mixed up. Put them in the correct order and write the numbers in the boxes below.

1   Now I'll just check that we've got it in the right place, so I'm going to pass just a little bit of air into the tube and listen to it. Can you let me listen to your stomach, please?

2   OK, can you sit forward on your chair, please? That's it! Now can you just lift your head a little? That's fine! Now I'm just going to mark the length of tube we need with this tape. That's it.

3   Yes, that seems fine. Well done!

Now I'll just put a little bit of tape over the tube to hold it in place. That's it! All over. You can relax now.

4   Now just a little spray in your left nostril. That's fine! Now if you want me to stop at any time just raise your hand. OK? Right, now here comes the first bit. You're doing very well.

5   Hello Mrs Turner. I'm Amy Nathan.

6   Now, can you just bend your head forward a little and I'd like you to take a sip of water through this straw. Fine!

7   Now, you're going to have an operation tomorrow and we need to make sure that your stomach is empty. What I'd like to do is slide a thin plastic tube through your nose and down into your stomach.

8   You're doing very well. Now, take another sip. That's it. And now another. Good. We're almost there. Well done!

9   Now, don't worry it won't cause you any pain, but it will feel a bit uncomfortable. It's not the most pleasant of things but we'll take it carefully. Are you OK about this?

5								

It's very important to keep talking calmly to the patient while carrying out such a procedure. The dialogue above gives several things you can say.

34 Communication skills

What function do the following sentences/phrases have? One example is given for each function.

1 Yes, of course.

2 It'll be OK. We'll make sure you have all the support you need.

3 I'm afraid the results of the tests are not good.

4 When you say you feel sick do you mean you want to vomit?

5 I think I can begin to understand how you feel.

6 Can you give me that number again, please?

7 I'm sorry but that's not the way I see it.

8 No, quite!

9 I've come today to discuss the results of your tests.

10 I'm sorry! I said the thirteenth not the thirtieth!

11 So, from what you've told me you suffer stomach pains, especially in the evenings, and have difficulties sleeping!

A STATING THE PURPOSE

I'd like to go over what we're going to do tomorrow. *9*

B CLARIFYING INFORMATION

Did you say these pains always come an hour after you've been eating?

C ASKING FOR REPETITION

Could you repeat that, please?

D SHOWING THAT YOU'RE LISTENING

Yes, I see!

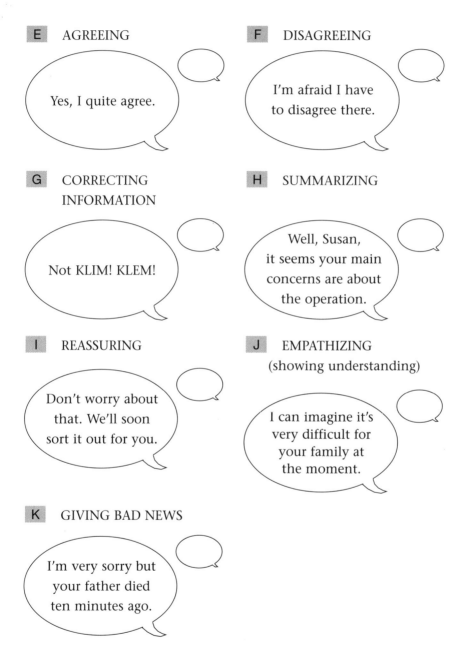

E AGREEING

Yes, I quite agree.

F DISAGREEING

I'm afraid I have to disagree there.

G CORRECTING INFORMATION

Not KLIM! KLEM!

H SUMMARIZING

Well, Susan, it seems your main concerns are about the operation.

I REASSURING

Don't worry about that. We'll soon sort it out for you.

J EMPATHIZING (showing understanding)

I can imagine it's very difficult for your family at the moment.

K GIVING BAD NEWS

I'm very sorry but your father died ten minutes ago.

It's important in English to choose your words carefully and to use polite phrases. Medical personnel are seldom criticized for their medical abilities but often criticized for their poor bedside manner (tact and sensitivity)!

35 Things on the ward

Write the number of each description next to the correct word.

sheets	_10_	oxygen point	____
mattress	____	urine bottle	____
crutch	____	hoist	____
trolley	____	wheelchair	____
vase	____	pillow	____
curtain	____	call button	____
drip stand	____	blanket	____
bedpan	____	basin	____
tray	____	name band	____
bedspread	____	monkey pole	____
observations chart	____		

1 This covers the bed to keep off the dust.

2 To rest their head on.

3 A patient confined to bed will have to use this to urinate and defecate.

4 Patients use this when they need to call a nurse.

5 For identification, this is worn by patients around their wrist.

6 A narrow bed for transporting patients.

7 Wash your hands here.

8 A mechanical device for lifting and moving patients.

9 Drawn around a patient's bed to provide some privacy.

10 Two of these on the bed are straightened regularly and washed every few days.

11   Meals are brought to the bed on this.

12   These keep the patient warm.

13   Male patients confined to bed use this to urinate.

14   Suspended above the bed, this can be used by the patient to pull herself up.

15   Patients lie on this, it's sometimes hard and sometimes soft!

16   Intravenous fluid bags are suspended on this.

17   Patients who can sit up comfortably can be transported in one of these.

18   A patient with a broken leg will need two of these to get around.

19   For flowers.

20   A mask and tube from this will supply oxygen to the patient.

21   The patient's condition is recorded here.

36 Equipment

Write the number of each piece of equipment next to the correct word.

scissors   _4_

forceps   _____

examination light   _____

scalpel   _____

weighing scales   _____

vaginal speculum   _____

syringe   _____

tongue depressor   _____

kidney dish   _____

stethoscope   _____

needle   _____

thermometer   _____

catheter   _____

medicine pot   _____

cotton wool   _____

tourniquet   _____

sterile latex gloves   _____

adhesive tape   _____

intravenous cannula   _____

dressing pack   _____

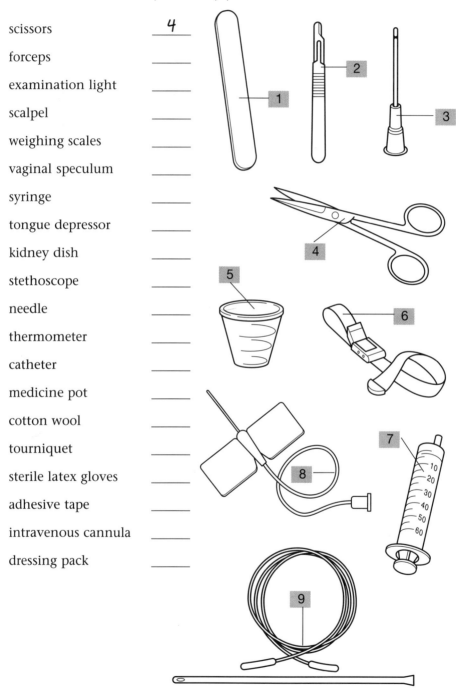

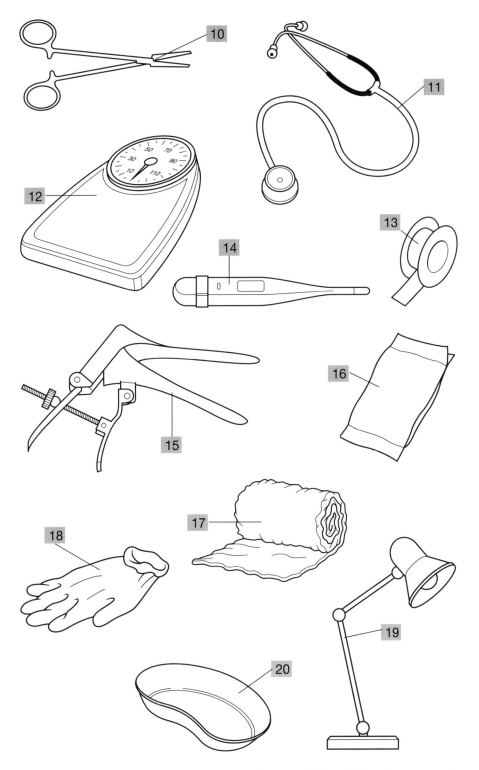

37 Types of illness

Replace the words in bold type (1–26) with a word from the list a–z. Write the letters in the grid.

a	ischaemia	b	defects	c	side effects
d	trauma	e	allergic	f	foetus
g	immunological	h	hereditary	i	idiosyncratic
j	benign	k	carrier	l	~~congenital~~
m	necrosis	n	contagious	o	degenerative
p	corrosive	q	neoplasms	r	protozoa
s	metabolic	t	epidemic	u	malignant
v	infectious	w	deficiency	x	obstruction
y	infestation	z	allergen		

A (1) **dating from birth** disease may be (2) **passed down from parents to offspring** or may be the result of damage to the (3) **unborn baby**. (4) **Physical damage** may be the result of surgical operations, accidents, excessive temperatures, radiation or (5) **destructive** chemicals. Mechanical (6) **faults** lead to the (7) **blocking** of tubes or vessels.

An infection or (8) **invasion** of living organisms may be the cause of disease. These living organisms include viruses, bacteria, (9) **worm-like parasites**, fungi or animal parasites. Some of these diseases are (10) **spread easily between people** and the result may be a (11) **large number of people suffering the disease**. It's possible to have a (12) **person with the disease but no symptoms**. Some diseases may be (13) **passed on by touching**. Most tumours are (14) **new growths**. Some of these are (15) **mild and self-limiting**, while others are (16) **cancerous and spread**.

A (17) **wearing out** disease happens when tissue loses its normal function. There may be (18) **insufficient blood supply to an organ** which may result in infarction and subsequent (19) **death of the tissue.**

If biochemical reactions in the body are upset, the result may be a (20) **chemical conversion** disease. One possible cause is an excess or (21) **shortage** of certain nutrients in the diet.

Problems in the body's complex defence mechanism can lead to (22) **defence mechanism** disease. One possible cause is a (23) **hypersensitive** reaction to an (24) **external substance** which to most people is harmless.

Some drugs or poisons may cause disease because of the (25) **unwanted action** of these drugs. This can be dose-related or (26) **have a bad effect only on a few people.**

1	2	3	4	5	6	7	8	9	10	11	12	13
I												
14	15	16	17	18	19	20	21	22	23	24	25	26

38 Diseases

Match the common name for a disease with its medical equivalent.

Medical name		Common name
alopecia	_baldness_	German measles
arteriosclerosis	_____	polio
bursitis	_____	thrush
candida	_____	warts
cerebral palsy	_____	heart attack
cerebral infarction/ bleeding	_____	heat spots/nettle rash
dyspepsia	_____	cold sore
eructation	_____	swelling
erythema pernio	_____	(to be) spastic
flatulence	_____	belching
haemorrhoids	_____	glandular fever
halitosis	_____	heartburn
herpes simplex	_____	~~baldness~~
herpes zoster	_____	chickenpox
hordeolum	_____	hardening of the arteries
infectious mononucleosis	_____	measles
myocardial infarction	_____	bad breath
oedema	_____	indigestion
poliomyelitis	_____	housemaid's knee
pyrosis	_____	piles
rubella	_____	shingles
rubeola; morbilli	_____	tennis elbow
tendonitis	_____	stroke
urticaria	_____	chilblains
varicella	_____	stye
verrucae	_____	wind

39 Infectious diseases: word building 2

The words on the right can be used to form a noun that fits suitably in the blank space. Fill each blank in this way.

1   The _sterilization_ of equipment is necessary to kill spores.   STERILE

2   Safe practice includes the safe _____ of waste.   DISPOSE

3   Hands must be carefully washed after _____   CONTAMINATE
    with body fluids.

4   A patient with a highly infectious disease may have   ISOLATE
    to be cared for in _____

5   Some disease organisms may trigger an inflammatory   RESPOND
    _____ in the body.

6   The _____ of influenza depends on the strain   SEVERE
    of virus causing it.

7   In the case of mumps the period of _____   INCUBATE
    is very long.

8   In most European countries, _____ against   VACCINATE
    many childhood diseases is available.

9   A long _____ is often required after   CONVALESCE
    glandular fever.

10 Many viral diseases are known to cause _____   INFLAME
    of the tonsils.

11 A programme of _____ has made diphtheria   IMMUNE
    a very rare disease in Britain.

12 Tetanus is an _____ by the Clostridium tetani bacillus.   INFECT

13 Typhoid fever is spread by _____ of food or   INGEST
    drink contaminated by bacillus from infected faeces.

14 If plaque is not removed from teeth it may lead to the   DESTROY
    _____ of the enamel.

Most of the nouns above end in -tion. Other suffixes which form nouns
above are -al, -ity, -ence, although -al is normally used to form adjectives
(industrial, economical). Try to think of some other nouns formed with these
suffixes. See also: Test 58.

40 Prepositions

Fill in the missing prepositions in the sentences below. Choose from the following. Some of the prepositions are used more than once.

about	against	by	down	from	in
	into	of	on	to	with

1 Disease can spread to another person through direct contact
   __with__ the patient.

2 Infection may be carried in water contaminated _____ sewage.

3 Malaria is transmitted _____ the bite of a mosquito.

4 Toxins released _____ the blood circulation may produce fever.

5 A rash is probably due _____ a viral infection.

6 The severity of the disease depends _____ the particular viral
   strain.

7 A secondary infection can be treated _____ appropriate
   antibiotics.

8 There are six patients suffering _____ 'flu'.

9 Patients must be warned _____ the dangers of secondary
   infection.

10 The measles rash appears _____ the forehead and then spreads
    _____ the body.

11 The German measles rash consists _____ pink macules.

12 Girls should be vaccinated _____ rubella if they have never had it.

13 Laryngeal spasm may cause difficulty _____ swallowing.

14 Antibiotics are effective _____ the Bordetella pertussis bacillus.

15 In the past many people died _____ smallpox.

16 Children are routinely immunized _____ polio, whooping cough and other diseases.

17 Typhoid fever is caused _____ Salmonella typhi.

18 Precautions must be taken to prevent the spread _____ infection.

19 Children are often concerned _____ a rash on their skin.

41 Genetics

In each set of three sentences, the same word is missing. Supply the word.

1   __chromosome__

Each _____ has another one exactly like it.

It's the sex _____ which determines an individual's sex.

The Y _____ is responsible for male characteristics.

2   _____

_____ is caused by an extra chromosome.

A foreshortened head, upward slanting eyes and a flat nasal bridge are some of the characteristic physical features of

_____ .

The chance of a women having a baby with _____ increases considerably with age.

3   _____

_____ is enclosed in the central nucleus of the cell.

The whole nature of a cell depends on the kinds of

_____ .

During division of a cell, the _____ duplicates itself.

4   _____

Brown eyes are _____ over blue eyes.

If one parent has a _____ characteristic from both his/her parents, he/she must pass it on to his/her children.

Gregor Mendel discovered that tall pea plants were

_____ .

5   _____

Each individual has a unique set of genes _____ from the parents.

Sickle cell disease is an _____ disease of the blood.

There is a chance of 1 in 4 that cystic fibrosis will be _____ by a second child born to parents of a child with the disease.

6 _____

Some diseases tend to run in families without observing any known rules of _____ .

With some diseases the effects of _____ and environment cannot always be distinguished.

The material from which chromosomes are formed governs

_____ .

7 _____

The child of normal parents may be affected by _____ in an ovum or a sperm.

A sudden change in the genetic makeup of an organism is known as _____ .

_____ leads to people being born with a defect.

8 _____

A sex-linked _____ transmits haemophilia.

Sickle-cell anaemia is the result of a defective recessive

_____ .

In Britain, the commonest disease due to a single pair of recessive _____s is cystic fibrosis.

9 _____

The chance that a child will be born with a serious _____ defect is 1 in 50.

Some _____ disorders can be cured.

_____ engineering has provided a plentiful supply of insulin.

42 Food

Fill in the missing words in the text below. Choose from the following.

absorbed	amino acids	amounts	~~balanced~~	bioavailable
cellulose	cereals	energy	fish	flavour	haemoglobin
healing	insulation	intake	iodine	lost	minerals	protect
pulses	riboflavin	starches	stored	undernutrition

A (1) __*balanced*__ diet contains all the necessary substances required by body cells. There can be adverse effects from overeating as well as from (2) _____ . A varied diet is the best way to ensure an adequate (3) _____ of all the essential nutrients. The essential nutrients are water, carbohydrate, protein, lipid, vitamins and (4) _____ .

Carbohydrates are the main source of (5) _____ . They comprise sugars, (6) _____ and complex polysaccharides. Fruit and vegetables provide carbohydrate but leaves and stalks can be indigestible because they contain more (7) _____ .

The component (8) _____ of protein are essential for structural maintenance, physiological regulation and energy supply. High quality protein which is easily digested and (9) _____ is found in meat, eggs, milk and fish and (10) _____ (beans, peas, lentils etc.).

Lipids provide concentrated energy and are used by the body to store energy. They provide (11) _____ under the skin, (12) _____ major organs from trauma and are required for effective neural function. They give food aroma and (13) _____ , increase palatability and give a feeling of satiety.

Only small (14) _____ of vitamins are required. Fat-soluble vitamins are absorbed from the small intestine and are found in (15) _____ and plant oils. They can be (16) _____ in the liver and adipose tissue. Water-soluble vitamins are easily (17) _____ from the body. Vitamin B complex includes thiamine, (18) _____ and nicotinic acid. Foods providing these include (19) _____ (wheat, rye) yeast, milk and eggs.

There are many minerals that are essential for health, but iron, (20) _____ , and zinc are the most significant. Zinc is involved in enzyme reactions and is important during periods of growth and wound (21) _____ . It is found in animal products. Iron is a major component of (22) _____ and is important in enzyme processes and in the immune response. Iron is found in most foods but must be in (23) _____ form.

43 Prefixes and suffixes

A What do the prefixes mean? Choose from the words in the box. You will have to use two of them twice.

> fat   milk   potassium   sodium   starch   stone   sugar   ~~water~~

	Prefix	Example	Meaning
1	hydro-	hydrotherapy	treatment with ___*water*___
2	lact-	lactation	formation of _____
3	racchar-	saccharine	like _____
4	amyl-	amylase	enzyme for digesting _____
5	steat-	steatogenous	producing _____
6	adip-	adipose	contains _____
7	glyc-	glycoside	derivative of _____
8	natr-	hypernatraemia	excess _____ in the blood
9	kal-	kaliuresis	secretion of _____ in urine
10	calc-	calculus	a _____

B What do the suffixes mean? Choose from the box.

> derivative   enzyme   precursor   substance   sugar

	Suffix	Meaning	Example
11	-ose	a _____	glucose, lactose
12	-ase	an _____	lactase, enterokinase
13	-ide	_____ of sugar	disaccharide, glycoside
14	-in	any kind of _____	pepsin, glycerine
15	-gen	a _____	pepsinogen, trypsinogen

 Test 4 also tests various prefixes used in medicine.

44 How's the patient: phrasal verbs

Complete the phrasal verbs in the following sentences by choosing a preposition/adverb from the box. You will have to use some of them more than once.

ahead	along	back	down	on	out	to

1 The operation has certainly brought him __*back*__ to health.

2 The medication will help bring _____ his blood pressure.

3 She fainted but quickly came _____ .

4 You're coming _____ fine. We'll have you home in no time!

5 She couldn't remember anything of the accident but slowly it's coming _____ to her.

6 We've cut _____ the growth and the wound should heal quickly.

7 She's done something _____ her back. She's having difficulties moving.

8 We're still trying to find _____ what is causing the high temperature.

9 She has decided to go _____ with the operation.

10 Several patients have gone _____ with a stomach bug.

11 Try to keep _____ this diet for the next four weeks.

12 The baby is growing quickly and putting _____ weight.

B Now match the phrasal verb with its meaning.

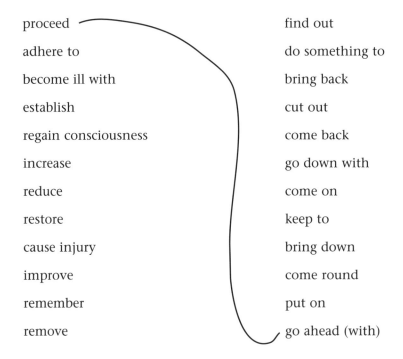

proceed	find out
adhere to	do something to
become ill with	bring back
establish	cut out
regain consciousness	come back
increase	go down with
reduce	come on
restore	keep to
cause injury	bring down
improve	come round
remember	put on
remove	go ahead (with)

Phrasal verbs are commonly used in spoken English but seldom used in formal written English. It's important to realize that a phrasal verb often has a particular meaning which differs from the verb used on its own. See also: Test 28.

45 The patient's condition

Fill in the missing verbs in the sentences below. You will have to change four of them into the correct tense! Choose from the box.

---

alleviate~~ cure experience heal immobilize improve
paralyse recover rehabilitate reject relapse relieve
respond resuscitate revive stabilize

---

1 The doctor has given her some medication to _alleviate_ the pain.

2 The operation was a success and we hope her body won't _____ the new heart.

3 It'll take up to six months to _____ fully from the hysterectomy.

4 We're very pleased with her condition. She's _____ well to treatment.

5 He's in intensive care at the moment where we're trying to _____ his condition.

6 At the scene of the accident the paramedics tried to _____ the casualty whose breathing had stopped.

7 It took some time to _____ her after she fainted.

8 Paracetamol will _____ the symptoms of the common cold but it won't _____ it.

9 If you leave the wound uncovered it will _____ more quickly.

10 The occupational therapist is working to _____ the patient after her serious accident.

11 The plaster cast acts to _____ the arm while the bone regrows.

12 Trauma to his spine has _____ his left leg.

13 Now that we have isolated the pathogen and can treat her, her condition should _____ rapidly.

14 He has made a good recovery but he still _____ occasional pain in his thigh.

15 He was making a good recovery but this morning he _____ and we have moved him to intensive care.

46 Seen on the skin

Write the number of each picture next to the correct word.

blister	_8_
boil	____
corn	____
cut	____
mole	____
bruise	____
rash	____
sunburn	____
acne	____
chilblains	____
scratch	____
graze	____
freckles	____
scar	____
birthmark	____

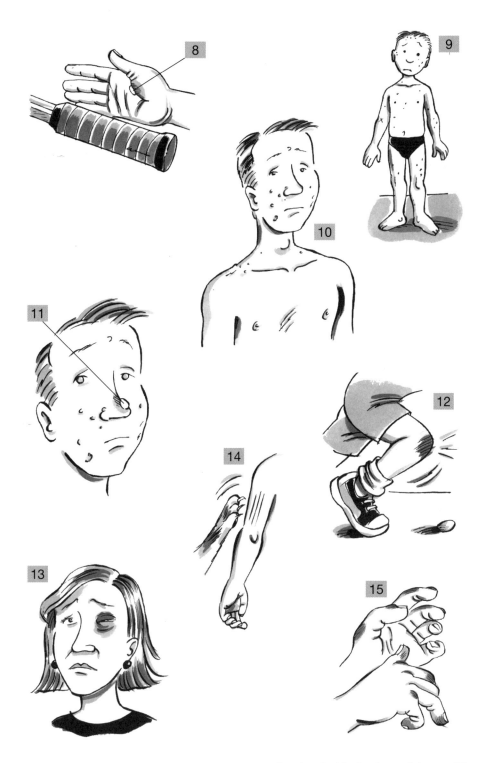

47 Heart and blood disorders

Fill in the crossword.

Across

5 Irregularities in the heartbeat.

7 Turbulent blood flow through a defective valve makes this sound.

9 A healthy heart has 60–100 of these a minute.

12 Coronary heart disease is due to _____ supply of blood to the heart.

15 The surgeon does this when he joins a piece of vein to the heart.

17 Atherosclerosis is a build up of fatty _____.

18 A completely new heart!

20 Insufficient _____ and smoking can contribute to heart disease.

23 A gripping angina chest pain sometimes _____ down the arms.

24 Air or liquid are used to _____ the balloon in angioplasty.

25 A section of the patient's saphenous vein is normally used in _____ surgery.

Down

1 The opposite of widening.

2 Complete stoppage of the heart.

3 Inflammation of the heart muscle.

4 Tachycardia is a rapid _____.

6 Death of a muscle due to lack of blood.

8 Battery-operated device to make the heart beat normally.

10 _____ veins are caused by defective valves in deep lower leg veins.

11 Angina pectoris chest pains are usually brought on by _____.

13 Platelets and blood cells which collect on one site will cause this.

14 The person who provides a replacement heart.

16 One of these in a coronary artery will cause the muscle it supplies to die.

19 Abnormal swelling in a weakened arterial wall.

21 A condition in which a valve outlet is too narrow.

22 It thickens arterial walls and narrows the artery.

48 Disorders of the digestive system

What is the doctor describing to the patient? Choose from the box.

cholangitis   cholecystectomy   cirrhosis   colonoscopy
Crohn's disease   diverticulitis   gastritis   haemorrhoids
~~hiatus hernia~~   irritable bowel syndrome   partial gastrectomy
peptic ulcer   pseudocyst   volvulus

1   *hiatus hernia*   2

> Because the muscles of the diaphragm are weak, a small part of the stomach has come through it.

> What we're going to do is remove the part of the stomach which is diseased.

3   4

> The combination of alcohol and smoking is causing inflammation of the stomach lining.

> The acids in the stomach have attacked the stomach lining and burrowed into the wall.

5   6

> The liver has been seriously damaged by too much alcohol.

> This is a small sac between the pancreas and the stomach which has filled with fluid.

7 _____

> A gall stone from the gallbladder has become stuck in the narrow tube and caused infection of the bile duct.

8 _____

> Because of the long history of problems with gallstones, it would be best to remove the gallbladder.

9 _____

> Some parts of the intestine have narrowed and some parts are inflamed and this means that food is not being properly absorbed.

10 _____

> Little pouches have been pushed through weak parts of the intestinal wall and become infected and swollen.

11 _____

> The barium X-ray shows that the intestine is normal. A change of diet may help relieve the feelings of bloating, wind and discomfort.

12 _____

> We're going to pass a thin, flexible tube through the back passage so we can see what's causing blood in the faeces.

13 _____

> The intestine has become a bit twisted and is now blocked.

14 _____

> These are swollen blood vessels that are protruding from the lining of the rectum.

When you are describing conditions or procedures to a patient you should use everyday language and avoid medical terminology which the patient is unlikely to understand. Practise making simple descriptions of medical conditions or procedures which you use. See also: Test 34.

49 Disorders of the skeletal system

Match up the definition with the correct term.

1 A break in a bone.

2 A crack in the surface of a bone.

3 With this kind of break, bones are forced from their normal anatomical position.

4 Following a break, this may be used to stop bones moving.

5 This can be used together with screws when a bone is badly broken in several places.

6 The force used to pull bones back into alignment.

7 There is a loss of this as people grow older.

8 Osteomalacia in children is known as this.

9 This disease is also known as osteitis deformans.

10 Osteoarthritis in the spine is the erosion of these intervertebral structures.

11 An abnormal curve of the spine may be due to this.

12 This injury is usually the result of a car accident when the neck is suddenly forced forward and then backward.

13 This injury is the partial tearing of a ligament.

14 A drastic shift of two bone ends out of their normal position.

15 With this condition uric acid collects in a synovial joint forming crystals.

16 An artificial joint.

17 A surgeon performing a hip joint replacement operation uses this instrument to shape the cavity in the pelvic bone for the femoral head.

a Paget's
b cast
c rickets
d fracture
e sprain
f gout
g prosthesis
h displaced
i whiplash
j reamer
k metal plate
l fissure
m discs
n bone mass
o dislocation
p traction
q bad posture

1	2	3	4	5	6	7	8	9	10	11	12	13	14	15	16	17
d																

50 Disorders of the nervous system

Complete the words in the following sentences by adding a prefix. Choose from the following. Some can be used more than once.

ab-   de-   dis-   im-   in-   ir-   un-

1 An epileptic seizure is _un_ controlled, chaotic electrical activity in the brain. It alters consciousness and may bring on ____voluntary movements. Epilepsy may be the result of chemical ____balance but more often the cause is ____known.

2 In a grand mal epileptic seizure, the victim falls to the ground ____conscious and makes twitching movements which may last for several minutes. In a petit mal seizure, the victim may be ____aware of things around him for up to thirty seconds but seldom loses consciousness.

3 In temporal lobe epilepsy, a seizure may result in the victim having ____rational feelings of anger or fear.

4 One of the most common ____abling disorders of the nervous system among young people is multiple sclerosis.

5 Parkinson's disease is a ____generative condition of the brain causing weakness and stiffness of the muscles.

6 People with dementia lose their memory of recent events and become ____interested in their appearance. In the later stages of dementia, patients may become bedridden and ____continent.

7 Alzheimer's disease shows an ____normal production of the protein amyloid.

8 Some drugs can slow the progress of Alzheimer's disease but it is ____curable.

9 Following a stroke, many patients are left with some sort of ____ability.

10 Brain cells starved of blood are ____able to communicate with the parts of the body they are responsible for.

11 A blow to the head could prove fatal if internal bleeding goes ____detected.

The prefixes used above make a word negative. There are few rules, but *ir-* is used before a word beginning with **r**. See also: Test 19.

51 Respiratory disorders

Rearrange the letters in brackets to form the correct word.

1   Pleural effusion can cause excess ____*fluid*____ to build up between the two pleura membrane layers. (diful)

2   A child with tonsillitis may find it difficult to _____ . (wolwals)

3   Lung cancer may be the result of inhaled _____ such as coal dust, asbestos and tobacco smoke. (ritritsan)

4   In the majority of cases of lung cancer, the _____ begins to grow in the bronchi. (urotmu)

5   A patient suffering from bronchitis may have a cough and feel breathless and their voice may be _____ . (sehoar)

6   A cough is the body's way of clearing excess _____ . (ucsmu)

7   Emphysema is a condition where the alveoli become overstretched and then _____ . (peturru)

8   A common cold frequently leads to a _____ nose. (dongsceet)

9   Drugs to treat asthma may be administered in a _____ which disperses the drug as a fine mist. (rebuilzen)

10 Mast-cell _____ are given to inhibit histamine production by the mast cells. (blaizsteirs)

11 Asbestosis is one disease caused by inhaling _____ _____ which lead to irreversible _____ . (stud stiplcare) (singcrar)

12 Asbestosis and silicosis are examples of _____ diseases resulting from a work environment. (countplacaio)

13 Increased sponginess of the nail bed, an increase in the curve of a nail and increased bulk over the terminal phalanges are physical signs of finger _____ . Many patients showing these signs have pulmonary disease. (blugcinb)

14 When collapsed small airways open during inspiration, short explosive sounds called _____ can be heard. (slecarck)

52 Disorders of the reproductive system

A doctor is talking to a patient. Match up the beginning of sentences 1–12 with the appropriate ending a–l to form twelve true sentences and write the letters in the table below.

1	I'd like you to go for a mammogram,	**a** so the uterus has dropped a bit.
2	I'm going to remove the tumour	**b** there is cancer of the right testicle.
3	I feel the heavy periods and discomfort which you're experiencing	**c** has enlarged in men over the age of fifty.
4	The ligaments that hold the uterus in place have become rather stretched,	**d** which is a simple X-ray of the breast.
5	After the hysterectomy operation you can expect	**e** I feel we should try to draw it out.
6	I'm going to use a laparoscope which is a very thin flexible viewing tube	**f** should provide some relief from the pain and discomfort.
7	Quite a bit of fluid has accumulated around the testis and	**g** I think we should carry out tests to confirm that you are ovulating.
8	The ultrasound scan has confirmed that	**h** together with a small area of the surrounding tissue.
9	It's quite common to find that the prostate gland	**i** due to a rather serious bacterial infection of the urethra.
10	The pain you've been experiencing on urination is	**j** to make a good recovery within five or six weeks.
11	I'd like to start you on a course of acyclovir for genital herpes but aspirin and warm salty baths	**k** are being caused by several large fibroids.
12	As you've been trying to conceive for some time now	**l** to examine the abdominal cavity.

1	2	3	4	5	6	7	8	9	10	11	12
d											

It's important not to cause offence or upset by giving information too directly. English uses qualifiers (*a bit*, *rather*, *simple*, *quite a bit of*) and phrases (*I think*, *I feel*) as well as modal verbs (*should*) to reduce the impact of the message and lessen anxiety.

53 Different types of drugs

Use the clues to fill in the missing letters to complete the names of types of drugs below.

#												
1			A	N	A	L	G	E	S	I	C	S
2			D									
3			M									
4			I-									
5			N									
6			I-									
7			S									
8			T									
9			E									
10			R									
11			A									
12			D									
13			R									
14			U									
15			G									

1   A wide range of drugs to relieve pain.

2   They help to remove excess fluid from the body.

3   They increase activity.

4   These drugs are used to reduce and suppress swelling.

5   Excellent painkillers originally derived from opium.

6   These help suppress nausea and vomiting.

7   One of the best known drugs which anyone can buy and use to relieve pain, inflammation and fever.

8   They prevent blood clots forming.

9   They soothe patients and help them sleep.

10   These are used to calm people and relieve anxiety.

11   Taken to relieve constipation.

12   These help to clear a stuffy nose.

13   Antibiotics are sometimes given this name because of the rapid relief they bring to many infectious diseases.

14   It's used in the treatment of diabetes.

15   It's used to increase the performance of a weak heart.

 All drugs which have been licensed and which are available on the National Health Service in Great Britain are listed in the *British National Formulary (BNF)*. The United States also has its own *National Formulary*. Is there an equivalent listing where you work?

54 The effects of drugs

Choose a suitable verb from the box to complete the phrases below. Use each one once only.

> alleviate   be absorbed   cause   dilate   have   impair   interfere
> ~~promote~~   reduce   soothe   stimulate   suppress   replace

_____*promote*_____	sleep
_____	into the blood stream
_____	the production of hormones
_____	with other drugs
_____	nausea
_____	an inhibitory effect
_____	the ability to drive
_____	the blood vessels
_____	side effects
_____	the heart rate
_____	pain
_____	inflammation
_____	abnormal losses of body fluids

Certain words tend to be used together to form a phrase. These are known as collocations and the exercise that you have just completed shows examples of collocations (*promote sleep*, *alleviate pain*). There is another collocations exercise in Test 15.

55 Giving instructions on drug administration

Complete the following sentences. Choose from the box. Some words may be used more than once.

apply	carry	chew	clean	continue	dip	dissolve	inhale
insert	lay	leave	put	~~rub~~	sip	spray	stick	take	wear

1. __rub__ a little of this ointment on his chest each morning.

2. _____ two of these tablets twice a day.

3. _____ two puffs in each nostril twice a day.

4. _____ the cream to the affected areas every morning.

5. Don't _____ these tablets. Swallow them whole.

6. _____ one pessary into the vagina before going to bed.

7. Ask your brother to help you _____ two drops into each ear in the morning.

8. It's best to _____ the patch on your thigh or lower back.

9. We would advise you to _____ these stockings until you're able to become a bit more active.

10. You should _____ this insulin kit with you at all times.

11. Just _____ the lozenge under the tongue and allow it to _____ slowly.

12. Make a hot drink and _____ it slowly.

13. _____ the wound with tepid water and _____ it open to the air.

14. _____ one teaspoonful in half a litre of hot water and _____ the steam.

15. _____ the end of the strip into the urine and wait to see if the colour changes.

16. Make sure you _____ with these pills until they're all finished, even if you think you're better!

56 Containers

Match up the following containers with the contents below.

1	a tube of _ointment_	8	a packet of _____
2	a jar of _____	9	a roll of _____
3	a bottle of _____	10	a _____ dispenser
4	a box of _____	11	a bar of _____
5	a vial of _____	12	a bag of _____
6	an ampoule of _____	13	a cartridge of _____
7	a tin of _____	14	a sachet of _____

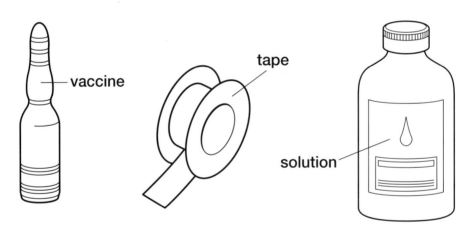

vaccine

tape

solution

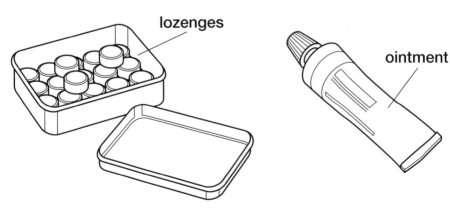

lozenges

ointment

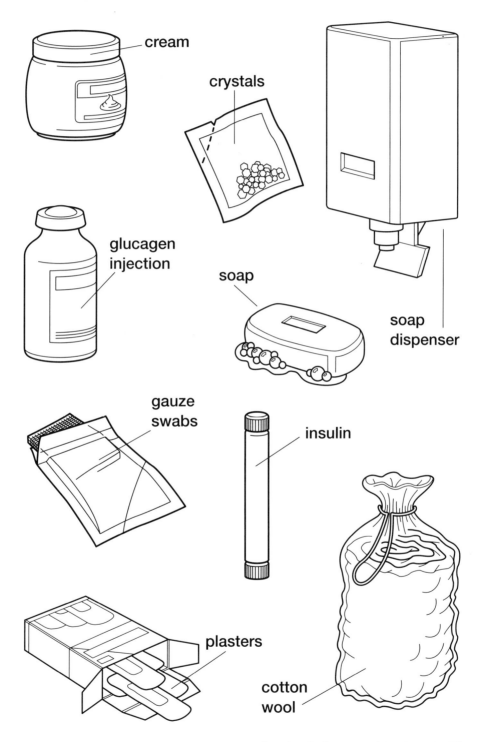

cream

crystals

glucagen
injection

soap

soap
dispenser

gauze
swabs

insulin

plasters

cotton
wool

57 Drug culture

What does a drug taker mean by the following? Choose the correct answer.

1 I need <u>a fix</u>!
   a) a pill
   b) time to lie down
   (c) an injection
   d) a tourniquet

2 He's <u>clean</u>!
   a) stopped taking drugs
   b) sells only pure drugs
   c) buys drugs
   d) conceals drugs by swallowing them

3 When did you <u>shoot up</u>?
   a) conceal drugs
   b) take an injection
   c) begin taking drugs
   d) buy drugs

4 He's <u>hooked</u>.
   a) preparing to inject
   b) addicted to drugs
   c) in prison
   d) in hospital

5 She takes <u>hard stuff</u>.
   a) sedatives
   b) LSD
   c) cocaine and opiates
   d) cannabis

6 Have you got <u>the machinery</u>?
   a) morphine
   b) supplier's phone number
   c) equipment for injecting
   d) a place to hide

7   She's <u>registered</u>.

a) obtains a regular prescription for drugs

b) is known by the police

c) knows where to buy drugs illegally

d) has been taken into hospital

8   I need <u>a script</u>!

a) a pack of clean needles

b) an injection

c) a pill

d) a prescription

9   Who's <u>the dealer</u>?

a) doctor

b) supplier

c) addict

d) heroin taker

10 She <u>does pipes</u>.

a) smokes crack cocaine

b) conceals drugs in the vagina

c) injects intravenously

d) inhales heroin fumes

11 He's a <u>junkie</u>.

a) heroin taker

b) stopped taking drugs

c) police informer

d) a doctor willing to prescribe drugs

There is a lot of language used by drug users which has a special meaning in the drug world. The language tested above includes some of the more common terms.

58 Surgery: word building 3

Use the word on the right to form a suitable word in each of the following sentences.

1. Gangrene in a foot may require the _amputation_ of the foot.   AMPUTATE

2. The _____ of all equipment used in the operating theatre is essential.   STERILE

3. A scalpel is a small _____ knife.   SURGERY

4. During surgery, the _____ administers drugs to prevent the patient feeling pain.   ANAESTHESIA

5. For some short operations, a local _____ may be given and the patient will be able to go home soon after.   ANAESTHESIA

6. One way of trying to diagnose an illness is to use _____ surgery.   EXPLORE

7. _____ surgery is required to cure a particular problem.   CORRECT

8. Certain conditions, which are not life threatening if left, can be treated with _____ surgery.   ELECT

9. Cosmetic surgery to improve appearance is usually _____ .   OPT

10. The surgeon tries to make the _____ along the lines of skin tension.   INCISE

11. _____ sutures don't need to be removed at a later date.   ABSORB

12. An operation may be carried out for the _____ of a tumour.   EXCISE

The list of patients who are going to theatre in one session is known as the **theatre list**. It must include the consultant's name, the theatre, the time when the list begins and the order of patients including each patient's name, age (date of birth), sex, ward, procedure (+side – left/right). See also: Test 39.

Write the number of each description next to the correct word.

retractors _15_	sterilizer ____	theatre gowns ____
scrub ____	respirator ____	dressing material ____
catheter ____	electrodes ____	drapes ____
swivel arm ____	suction ____	pedestal ____
flow metre ____	electrocardiograph ____	tray ____

1 This equipment keeps the patient breathing during surgery.

2 This allows the surgeon to move the lights easily into position.

3 This shows the anaesthetist the quantity of nitrous oxide or oxygen which is being given.

4 The operating table has no legs. It stands on a _____.

5 These are placed over wounds at the end of the operation.

6 Equipment is put in this to remove all germs.

7 Sterile instruments are placed and carried in this.

8 This equipment monitors heart activity.

9 These are attached to the patient's body to pick up heart activity.

10 These are worn by surgeons and nurses in theatre.

11 This is inserted to drain urine from the bladder.

12 The patient and trolleys in theatre are covered in sterile _____.

13 The _____ nurse provides instruments for the surgeon and assists when necessary during an operation.

14 This equipment is used to draw off any blood and body fluids during surgery.

15 These instruments hold open the site of operation during surgery.

The clothes worn by medical staff working in theatre are often referred to as *theatre greens* or *theatre blues* depending on the colours chosen by the individual hospital. It is quite common for theatre staff and recovery staff to wear different colours to distinguish them.

60 Giving advice

Complete the following pieces of advice. Choose from the box.

> It would be   You could try   We'd like   What about   You may find
> Have you   I strongly suggest that   You should try to
> Please don't   You'll recover more quickly   You must keep
> It would be good   Don't hesitate to   Do you think you could

1   ___Please don't___ strain your eyes by reading in poor light.

2   _____ eat more fresh fruit and vegetables.

3   _____ nicotine patches.

4   _____ all medicines out of reach of children.

5   _____ writing a letter to your sister?

6   _____ if you try to get some exercise.

7   _____ call us if her condition changes.

8   _____ a good idea to stop smoking.

9   _____ tried swimming?

10   _____ you to do these exercises every day.

11   _____ you reduce the amount of beer you drink.

12   _____ lose a bit of weight?

13   _____ it helpful to raise the head of your bed.

14   _____ for you to drink more water.

In English it's important to choose your words carefully so as not to upset or offend people. We often use *would*, *could* or *may* to lessen the impact of what we are saying or we offer advice in a polite question form. See also: Test 23.

Answers

Test 1

forehead 2	neck 31
chest 12	waist 17
big toe 28	chin 9
knee 26	throat 11
cheek 7	finger 22
palm 20	shoulder 32
ear 6	arm 14
back 33	breast 16
thigh 25	foot 30
thumb 21	wrist 19
stomach 18	armpit 13
mouth 8	groin 24
head 1	calf 27
ankle 29	bottom 34
hip 23	eye 4
eyebrow 3	jaw 10
elbow 15	nose 5

Test 2

1 skeletal system
2 reproductive system
3 integumentary system
4 endocrine system
5 cardiovascular system
6 digestive system
7 urinary system
8 somatic muscles
9 haematology
10 lymphatic system
11 nervous system
12 respiratory system

Test 3

1 h	6 g	11 m
2 n	7 f	12 j
3 b	8 o	13 k
4 d	9 a	14 c
5 i	10 e	15 l

Test 4

arm	brachi-
body	somat-, corpor-
breast	mast-, mamm-
cheek	bucca-
chest	thorac-, steth-, pect-
ear	ot-, aur-
eye	ophthalm-, ocul-
face	faci-
finger/toe	dactyl-, digit-
foot	pod-, ped-
hand	cheir-, man-
head	cephal-, capit-
mouth	stom(at)-, or-
neck	trachel-, cervic-
nose	rhin-, nas-
wrist	carp-

examples of words using these roots: brachiocephalic, somatic, superior corpora, hypermastia, submammary, buccal nerve, thoracic surgeon, stethoscope, pectoral muscle, otitis media, auriscalpium, ophthalmoscope, oculomotor nerve, brachiofaciolingual, arachnodactyly, digitigrade, podiatrist, pedicure, cheiroplasty, maniphalanx, encephalograph, capitate bone, stomatitis, intraoral, trachelopexy, cervical plexus, rhinitis, palatonasal, carpal bones.

Test 5

1 patients
2 admits, ward
3 referral
4 request
5 on-call
6 specimens
7 ward round
8 consent
9 discharged
10 outpatient, clinic
11 cover
12 convalescent
13 locum

Test 6

1	neoplastic	7	starvation
2	manifestations	8	asthma
3	pathogenesis	9	physical
4	ultrasound	10	infections
5	biopsy	11	cyanide
6	environment		

Test 7

1 blurry, double, unclear
2 anxious, confused, faint, tense
3 woozy, light, pounding, throbbing
4 numb, weak, tingling, stiff
5 wheezing, barking, hawking, husky
6 sweet, sour, bitter, salty
7 offensive, stinky, foul, nauseating
8 slimy, creamy, pinkish, transparent

Test 8

A

square, square
circle, circular
triangle, triangular
semicircle, semicircular
diamond, diamond-shaped
sphere, spherical
hemisphere, hemispherical
cylinder, cylindrical
cone, conical
pyramid, pyramidal

B

pear-shaped
S-shaped
heart-shaped
wedge-shaped
egg-shaped
disc-shaped
dome-shaped
horseshoe-shaped
fan-shaped
C-shaped
kidney-shaped
H-shaped

C

funnel-shaped = infundibulum
pear-shaped = uterus
dome-shaped = diaphragm
tubular = femur
hoop-shaped = atlas
tapering wedge-shaped = sacrum and coccyx
horseshoe-shaped = hyoid bone
pyramidal = orbit
C-shaped = bars of cartilage in the trachea

Test 9

Across

1 humerus
4 coccyx
7 hyoid
9 clavicle
11 incus
12 mandible
13 skull
17 phalanges
20 skeleton
21 elbow
22 patella
23 head
24 limbs
26 articulate
27 tibia
28 foot

Down

2 radius
3 synovial
5 orbit
6 collagen
8 backbone
10 ribs
14 cartilage
15 vertebra
16 ligaments
18 sternum
19 fovea
25 shaft

examples:

common name	*medical name*
collar bone	clavicle
anvil	incus
lower jaw	mandible
funny bone	elbow
knee cap	patella
shin bone	tibia
eye socket	orbit
backbone	spinal column
breast bone	sternum

Test 10

1 skeletal
2 flexible
3 resistant
4 cranial, facial
5 central
6 connective
7 collagenous
8 tubular
9 protective
10 cartilaginous
11 movable
12 lubricating
13 muscular
14 powerful
15 vertebral

examples:
-al: central, peripheral
-ible: reversible, edible
-ant: arrogant, recalcitrant
-ive: responsive, expensive
-ous: hazardous, dangerous
-ar: particular, similar
-ful: careful, forgetful
-ing: opposing, reducing
-ar: circular, triangular

Test 11

1. muscle, circulatory, pyramidal, cavity
2. communicate
3. vessels, arteries, veins
4. lungs, heart
5. oxygenated
6. pump, chambers, atria, wall, pumping, systemic, contraction, relaxation
7. valves, cusps, close
8. beats, pulse, wrist
9. branch, arterioles, capillaries

Test 12

A

mouth = buccal cavity
roof of the mouth = hard and soft palate
spit = saliva
throat = pharynx
gullet = oesophagus
small intestine = ileum
large intestine = colon
bowel = duodenum, jejunum, ileum, colon, and rectum

B

duodenum 14
large intestine 16
salivary gland 2
gullet 11
rectum 17
stomach 12
pancreas 13
appendix 7
gall bladder 4
caecum 6
mouth 1
liver 3
small intestine 15
roof of the mouth 8
anus 18
tongue 9
bile duct 5
throat 10

Test 13

1 i	6 o	11 n
2 g	7 a	12 f
3 m	8 l	13 j
4 k	9 e	14 h
5 c	10 b	15 d

Test 14

1. central
2. cranial
3. reflex
4. potential
5. receptor
6. effector
7. neurones
8. synapse
9. neurotransmitters
10. sensory, autonomous
11. dendrites, axon
12. grey matter
13. somatic
14. ganglion
15. automatic
16. sympathetic

Test 15

1. fallopian tubes
2. amniotic fluid
3. maternal blood
4. lanugo hair
5. birth canal
6. menstrual period
7. uterine contractions
8. multiple pregnancy
9. dilated cervix
10. breech position
11. foetal monitoring
12. umbilical cord
13. premature baby

Test 16

1. is eliminated
2. is separated
3. are called
4. are situated
5. are surrounded
6. is reflected
7. are retained
8. are pumped
9. are absorbed
10. is recovered
11. is altered
12. is set up
13. are formed
14. is lost
15. is transported
16. is stored
17. is felt

Test 17

1 breast	10 fertilization
2 embryo	11 vagina
3 prostate gland	12 nipple
4 ovary	13 penis
5 ovulation	14 puberty
6 vas deferens	15 menstruation
7 uterus	16 uterine tubes
8 lactation	17 pregnancy
9 testes	18 menopause

Test 18

A

hair 1
epidermis 2
subcutaneous fat 14
nerve fibre 11
sebaceous gland 3
arrector muscle 5
dermis 4
blood capillaries 12
pore 9
hair bulb 7
sweat gland 13
duct 10
hypodermis 8
hair follicle 6

B

1 d	5 e	9 g
2 k	6 j	10 a
3 f	7 c h l	
4 i	8 b	

Test 19

1 secreted
2 excite, inhibit
3 bind, buffer
4 fluctuate, continuous, intermittent
5 disequilibrium, consequences, overproduction, underproduction
6 stimulate
7 derive
8 metabolism, maintains
9 regulator, accelerates

Test 20

1 a	5 b	9 a
2 b	6 b	10 a
3 c	7 c	11 d
4 a	8 a	

Test 21

1 f	5 g	9 l
2 d	6 a	10 j
3 k	7 h	11 i
4 e	8 b	12 c

Test 22

1 f	6 m	11 b
2 l	7 c	12 i
3 d	8 e	13 g
4 a	9 n	14 k
5 h	10 j	

Test 23

1 Let's have a look at you! ('Let's' is followed by the infinitive of the verb.)
2 Could you just turn over, please? ('turn over' implies the body and it therefore is wrong to add this to the sentence.)
3 I'd like you to walk slowly across the room. ('I'd like you' is always followed by the infinitive of the verb with 'to'.)
4 Can you read the first letter on the board? (The modal verb 'can' is always used with the infinitive of the verb without 'to'.)
5 Would you just stand on the scales, please? ('Would' is used together with the infinitive of the verb without 'to'.)
6 Now try to press just a little bit harder.
7 I was wondering if you could show me your tummy? (*I was wondering if* is a very polite friendly request and could be used with adults as well as children.)
8 Would you like to just slip off your socks and shoes? ('Do you like to' is a question about likes and dislikes not a request.)
9 Would you mind waiting outside for a few moments? ('Would you mind' is always followed by -ing.)
10 Try hard to stay as still as possible! ('Try' is always followed by the infinitive of the verb with 'to'.)
11 So, you can put your things back on now!

12 Please tell me if you feel any discomfort. (A conditional sentence does not have 'will' in the conditional clause)

13 Do you think you could lie on your left side, please? ('could' does not indicate a request in this case.)

14 Could you possibly find someone to bring you to the clinic next week? (An adverb is placed before the main verb.)

Test 24

1	clench	11	stretch
2	show	12	touch
3	open	13	stand
4	lift	14	turn
5	take	15	close
6	say	16	lie
7	grip	17	hold
8	read	18	roll
9	cough	19	rest
10	bend	20	relax

Test 25

socks 9		laces 8
cardigan 17		collar 16
vest 19		jumper 25
jacket 11		shirt 13
boots 7		top 23
trousers 4		pocket 6
bra 21		sleeve 15
underpants 20		skirt 1
pyjamas 2		scarf 24
nightdress 10		zip 5
knickers 22		button 18
tie 12		cuff 14
hat 26		dressing gown 3

Test 26

A3: attend surgery in 3 days' time
AF: atrial fibrillation
A/G ratio: albumin/globulin ratio
AS: asthma
BOR: bowels open regularly
BP: blood pressure
° ↑ BP: no raised blood pressure
Cgh: cough
CO: Casualty Officer
C/O: complains of
CVS: cardiovascular system
D&C: dilation and curettage
DM: diabetes mellitus
DOB: date of birth
DVT: deep vein thrombosis
Ep: epilepsy
G and A: gas and air
HPC: history of present complaint
°JACCOL: no jaundice, anaemia, cyanosis, clubbing, oedema, lymphadenopathy
LBP: low back pain
°LKKS: no palpable liver, kidneys, spleen
MI: myocardial infarct
MRU: mass radiography unit
N&V: nausea and vomiting
OD: overdose
O/E: on examination
OPA: outpatient appointment
PM: post-mortem
PMH: past medical history
PR: per rectum
RS: respiratory system
Sat: satisfactory
SH: social history
SOB: short of breath
T: temperature
°TB: no tuberculosis
U/S: ultrasound
XR: X-ray

Test 27

1 cough, sore throat
2 out of breath
3 lost my appetite
4 can't sleep
5 runny nose, temperature
6 bruise
7 insect bite, swollen leg
8 headache, black eye
9 depressed
10 lump
11 nosebleed
12 stomach-ache

Test 28

1	b	6	c
2	d	7	b
3	c	8	c
4	a	9	d
5	d	10	a

Test 29

1. medical records
2. labour ward
3. theatre
4. laboratory
5. recovery area
6. corridor
7. canteen
8. mortuary
9. intensive care
10. accident and emergency
11. pharmacy
12. blood bank
13. coronary care unit
14. lift
15. geriatric ward

Test 30

1	e	9	d
2	k	10	p
3	f	11	i
4	j	12	h
5	l	13	c
6	o	14	g
7	a	15	m
8	b	16	n

Test 31

1	grateful	8	obstruction
2	persistently	9	response
3	respond	10	discomfort
4	nasal	11	drip
5	persist	12	examination
6	opinion	13	instance
7	findings	14	responds

Test 32

1	passed	10	tic
2	weight	11	break
3	site	12	borne
4	patience	13	check
5	bald	14	heal
6	faint	15	groan
7	lumbar	16	pitted
8	swabs	17	soar
9	waste		

Test 33

5 7 9 2 4 6 8 1 3

Test 34

A	9	E	1	I	2
B	4	F	7	J	5
C	6	G	10	K	3
D	8	H	11		

Test 35

sheets 10
oxygen point 20
mattress 15
urine bottle 13
crutch 18
hoist 8
trolley 6
wheelchair 17
vase 19
pillow 2
curtain 9
call button 4
drip stand 16
blanket 12
bedpan 3
basin 7
tray 11
name band 5
bedspread 1
monkey pole 14
observations chart 21

Test 36

scissors 4
forceps 10
examination light 19
scalpel 2
weighing scales 12
vaginal speculum 15
syringe 7
tongue depressor 1
kidney dish 20
stethoscope 11
needle 3
thermometer 14
catheter 9
medicine pot 5
cotton wool 17
tourniquet 6
sterile latex gloves 18
adhesive tape 13
intravenous cannula 8
dressing pack 16

Test 37

1 l	8 y	15 j	22 g
2 h	9 r	16 u	23 e
3 f	10 v	17 o	24 z
4 d	11 t	18 a	25 c
5 p	12 k	19 m	26 i
6 b	13 n	20 s	
7 x	14 q	21 w	

Test 38

alopecia = baldness
arteriosclerosis = hardening of the arteries
bursitis = housemaid's knee
candida = thrush
cerebral palsy = (to be) spastic
cerebral infarction/bleeding = stroke
dyspepsia = indigestion
eructation = belching
erythema pernio = chilblains
flatulence = wind
haemorrhoids = piles
halitosis = bad breath
herpes simplex = cold sore
herpes zoster = shingles
hordeolum = stye
infectious mononucleosis = glandular fever
myocardial infarction = heart attack
oedema = swelling
poliomyelitis= polio
pyrosis = heartburn
rubella = German measles
rubeola; morbilli = measles
tendonitis = tennis elbow
urticaria = heat spots/nettle rash
varicella = chickenpox
verrucae = warts

Test 39

1	sterilization	8	vaccination
2	disposal	9	convalescence
3	contamination	10	inflammation
4	isolation	11	immunization
5	response	12	infection
6	severity	13	ingestion
7	incubation	14	destruction

examples:
-tion: education, information
-al: removal, withdrawal
-ity: punctuality, similarity
-ence: insistence, persistence

Test 40

1	with	11	of
2	by	12	against
3	by	13	in
4	into	14	against
5	to	15	of/from
6	on	16	against
7	with	17	by
8	from	18	of
9	of/about	19	about
10	on, to/down		

Test 41

1 chromosome
2 Down's syndrome
3 DNA (deoxyribonucleic acid)
4 dominant
5 inherited
6 inheritance
7 mutation
8 gene
9 genetic

Test 42

1 balanced
2 undernutrition
3 intake
4 minerals
5 energy
6 starches
7 cellulose
8 amino acids
9 absorbed
10 pulses
11 insulation
12 protect
13 flavour
14 amounts
15 fish
16 stored
17 lost
18 riboflavin
19 cereals
20 iodine
21 healing
22 haemoglobin
23 bioavailable

Test 43
A
1 water	6 fat
2 milk	7 sugar
3 sugar	8 sodium
4 starch	9 potassium
5 fat	10 stone

B
11 sugar	14 substance
12 enzyme	15 precursor
13 derivative	

Test 44
1 back	7 to
2 down	8 out
3 to	9 ahead
4 along	10 down
5 back	11 to
6 out	12 on

proceed = go ahead (with)
adhere to = keep to
become ill with = go down with
establish = find out
regain consciousness = come round
increase = put on
reduce = bring down
restore = bring back
cause injury = do something to
improve = come on
remember = come back
remove = cut out

Test 45
1 alleviate	9 heal
2 reject	10 rehabilitate
3 recover	11 immobilize
4 responding	12 paralysed
5 stabilize	13 improve
6 resuscitate	14 experiences
7 revive	15 relapsed
8 relieve, cure	

Test 46
blister 8	acne 10
boil 11	chilblains 15
corn 4	scratch 14
cut 1	graze 12
mole 6	freckles 2
bruise 13	scar 3
rash 9	birthmark 7
sunburn 5	

Test 47
Across	Down
5 arrhythmias	1 narrowing
7 murmur	2 arrest
9 beats	3 myocarditis
12 restricted	4 pulse
15 grafts	6 infarction
17 deposits	8 pacemaker
18 transplant	10 varicose
20 exercise	11 exertion
23 radiates	13 clot
24 inflate	14 donor
25 bypass	16 blockage
	19 aneurysm
	21 stenosis
	22 plaque

Test 48
1 hiatus hernia
2 partial gastrectomy
3 gastritis
4 peptic ulcer
5 cirrhosis
6 pseudocyst
7 cholangitis
8 cholecystectomy
9 Crohn's disease
10 diverticulitis
11 irritable bowel syndrome
12 colonoscopy
13 volvulus
14 haemorrhoids

Test 49
1 d	7 n	13 e
2 l	8 c	14 o
3 h	9 a	15 f
4 b	10 m	16 g
5 k	11 q	17 j
6 p	12 i	

Test 50
1 uncontrolled, involuntary, imbalance, unknown
2 unconscious, unaware
3 irrational
4 disabling
5 degenerative
6 uninterested (some people may use disinterested), incontinent
7 abnormal
8 incurable

9 disability
10 unable
11 undetected

Test 51
1 fluid
2 swallow
3 irritants
4 tumour
5 hoarse
6 mucus
7 rupture
8 congested
9 nebulizer
10 stabilizers
11 dust particles, scarring
12 occupational
13 clubbing
14 crackles

Test 52

1	d	5	j	9	c
2	h	6	l	10	i
3	k	7	e	11	f
4	a	8	b	12	g

Test 53
1 analgesics
2 diuretics
3 stimulants
4 anti-inflammatory
5 narcotics
6 anti-emetics
7 aspirin
8 anticoagulants
9 sedatives
10 tranquillizers
11 laxatives
12 decongestants
13 miracle drugs
14 insulin
15 digitalis

Test 54
promote sleep
be absorbed into the blood stream
stimulate the production of hormones
interfere with other drugs
suppress nausea
have an inhibitory effect

impair the ability to drive
dilate the blood vessels
cause side effects
reduce the heart rate
alleviate pain
soothe inflammation
replace abnormal losses of body fluids

Test 55
1 rub (put)
2 take
3 spray (put)
4 apply
5 chew
6 insert (put)
7 put
8 stick (apply)
9 wear
10 carry (take)
11 lay, dissolve
12 sip
13 clean, leave
14 dissolve, inhale
15 dip
16 continue

Test 56
1 a tube of <u>ointment</u>
2 a jar of <u>cream</u>
3 a bottle of <u>solution</u>
4 a box of <u>plasters</u>
5 a vial of <u>glucagen injection</u>
6 an ampoule of <u>vaccine</u>
7 a tin of <u>lozenges</u>
8 a packet of <u>gauze swabs</u>
9 a roll of <u>tape</u>
10 a <u>soap</u> dispenser
11 a bar of <u>soap</u>
12 a bag of <u>cotton wool</u>
13 a cartridge of <u>insulin</u>
14 a sachet of <u>crystals</u>

Test 57

1	c	7	a
2	a	8	d
3	b	9	b
4	b	10	a
5	c	11	a
6	c		

Test 58

1	amputation	7	corrective
2	sterility	8	elective
3	surgical	9	optional
4	anaesthetist	10	incision
5	anaesthetic	11	absorbable
6	exploratory	12	excision

Test 59

retractors 15
scrub 13
catheter 11
swivel arm 2
flow metre 3
sterilizer 6
respirator 1
electrodes 9
suction 14
electrocardiograph 8
theatre gowns 10

dressing material 5
drapes 12
pedestal 4
tray 7

Test 60

1 Please don't
2 You should try to
3 You could try
4 You must keep
5 What about
6 You'll recover more quickly
7 Don't hesitate to
8 It would be
9 Have you
10 We'd like
11 I strongly suggest that
12 Do you think you could
13 You may find
14 It would be good

Word list

The numbers after the entries are the tests in which they appear.

Test Your way to success in English

Test Your Professional English

0582 45163 9

0582 45148 5

0582 45149 3

0582 45160 4

0582 45161 2

0582 46898 1

0582 46897 3

0582 45150 7

0582 45147 7

0582 45162 0

www.penguinenglish.com